Jossey-Bass Teacher

$$2x - 5x + 6x = 3x \quad A(B + C) = AB + AC \quad 4 \times 5 = 5 \times 4 \quad 2(3 + 5)^2 + (-1)^2 \quad y = mx + b$$

Jossey-Bass Teacher provides educators with practical knowledge and tools to create a positive and lifelong impact on student learning. We offer classroom-tested and research-based teaching resources for a variety of grade levels and subject areas. Whether you are an aspiring, new, or veteran teacher, we want to help you make every teaching day your best.

From ready-to-use classroom activities to the latest teaching framework, our value-packed books provide insightful, practical, and comprehensive materials on the topics that matter most to K–12 teachers. We hope to become your trusted source for the best ideas from the most experienced and respected experts in the field.

Other titles in *Out Loud* series.
Algebra Out Loud
Geometry Out Loud

PRE-ALGEBRA OUT LOUD

$$2x - 5x + 6x = 3x \quad A(B + C) = AB + AC \quad 4 \times 5 = 5 \times 4 \quad 2(3 + 5)^2$$

Learning Mathematics Through Reading and Writing Activities

PAT MOWER

JOSSEY-BASS
A Wiley Imprint
www.josseybass.com

Published by Jossey-Bass
A Wiley Imprint
One Montgomery Street, Suite 1200, San Francisco, CA 94104-4594—www.josseybass.com

Jossey-Bass books and products are available through most bookstores. To contact Jossey-Bass directly call our Customer Care Department within the U.S. at 800-956-7739, outside the U.S. at 317-572-3986, or fax 317-572-4002.

Wiley also publishes its books in a variety of electronic formats and by print-on-demand. Not all content that is available in standard print versions of this book may appear or be packaged in all book formats. If you have purchased a version of this book that did not include media that is referenced by or accompanies a standard print version, you may request this media by visiting http://booksupport.wiley.com. For more information about Wiley products, visit us at www.wiley.com.

ISBN: 9780470539491
Printed in the United States of America
FIRST EDITION

PB Printing 10 9 8 7 6 5 4 3 2 1

Contents

$$2x - 5x + 6x = 3x \quad A(B + C) = AB + AC \quad 4 \times 5 = 5 \times 4 \quad 2(3 + 5)^2 + (-1)^2 \quad y = mx + b$$

About the Author   ix

Acknowledgments   xi

Introduction   xiii

1   The Basic Tools of Algebra   1

Mini-Lesson 1.1   The Big Ideas of Algebra   2

Activity 1.1   The Writing Is on the Wall   4

Activity 1.2   Semantic Word Maps   7

Activity 1.3   Math Glossary   10

Activity 1.4   Concept Circles   12

Mini-Lesson 1.2   Solving Simple Equations   16

Activity 1.5   Math Story   18

Activity 1.6   Algorithm Writing   20

Activity 1.7   One-Minute Summary   23

2   Exploring Infinite Sets   25

Mini-Lesson 2.1   Infinite Sets   26

Activity 2.1   Magic Square   28

Activity 2.2   One-Minute Summary   33

Mini-Lesson 2.2   Properties of the Real Numbers   34

Activity 2.3   Graphic Organizers   38

Activity 2.4   Reading Math Symbols   41

Activity 2.5   Math Glossary   43

Activity 2.6   Semantic Feature Analysis   45

Activity 2.7   In Your Own Words: A Paraphrasing Activity   49

3 Topics in Integers   53

Mini-Lesson 3.1   Egyptian Multiplication   54

Activity 3.1   The Writing Is on the Wall   57

Activity 3.2   Concept Cards   59

Activity 3.3   Frayer Model   61

Mini-Lesson 3.2   Integral Exponents   64

Activity 3.4   What's My Rule?   67

Activity 3.5   Comparison-and-Contrast Matrix   70

Activity 3.6   Knowledge Ratings   74

4 Number Theory   77

Mini-Lesson 4.1   Divisibility Rules   78

Activity 4.1   Number Riddles   81

Activity 4.2   In Your Own Words: A Paraphrasing Activity   84

Activity 4.3   Magic Square   86

Mini-Lesson 4.2   Greatest Common Denominator and Least Common Multiple   89

Activity 4.4   Semantic Feature Analysis   93

5 Fractions, Decimals, and Percents   99

Mini-Lesson 5.1   Pizza Math   100

Activity 5.1   What's My Rule?   102

Activity 5.2   Writing Prompts   104

Mini-Lesson 5.2   Conversions   106

Activity 5.3   Comparison-and-Contrast Matrix   108

Activity 5.4   Semantic Word Maps   111

6 Equations and Inequalities   115

Mini-Lesson 6.1   Solving Multistep Equations   116

Activity 6.1   In Your Own Words: A Paraphrasing Activity   118

Activity 6.2   Method of Operation   121

Mini-Lesson 6.2   Solving Linear Inequalities   123

Activity 6.3   Translating Words into Algebra   126

Activity 6.4   Writing Word Problems   128

Activity 6.5   Math Glossary   131

Activity 6.6   Biographies of Algebraists   133

7   Visualizing Algebra by Graphing Lines   137

Mini-Lesson 7.1   The xy-Plane and Lines   138

Activity 7.1   Muddiest Point   141

Activity 7.2   Reading and Understanding Graphs   143

Activity 7.3   K-W-L   146

Mini-Lesson 7.2   The Slope of a Line   149

Activity 7.4   Semantic Feature Analysis   151

Activity 7.5   Anticipation Guide   154

8   Geometry   157

Mini-Lesson 8.1   Plane Figures   158

Activity 8.1   Geometric Figure Description   161

Activity 8.2   Semantic Feature Analysis   165

Mini-Lesson 8.2   Pyramids and Prisms   168

Activity 8.3   Writing a Method of Operation   170

Activity 8.4   Math Story   175

Activity 8.5   In Your Own Words: A Paraphrasing Activity   179

Activity 8.6   Biographies of Geometers   181

References   185

About the Author

Pat Mower is an associate professor in the Department of Mathematics and Statistics at Washburn University in Topeka, Kansas. She earned her B.S. in mathematics and English at Dickinson University in Dickinson, North Dakota, and both her M.S. in mathematics and statistics and her Ph.D. in teacher education with emphasis in mathematics at the University of North Dakota. She is the author of three books on reading and writing to learn mathematics strategies and activities, all published by Jossey-Bass. Pat currently teaches Math for Middle School Educators, History of Math, Exploring Mathematics, and an online version of Exploring Mathematics. Her interests are in the history of mathematics and using ancient methods for solving problems and also in the pedagogy of freshman mathematics.

Acknowledgments

$$2x - 5x + 6x = 3x \quad A(B + C) = AB + AC \quad 4 \times 5 = 5 \times 4 \quad 2(3 + 5)^2 + (-1)^2 \quad y = mx + b$$

I am grateful for the patience and support of my husband, Derek; my mother who recently passed; my older brother, John C.; and my basset hounds, who were just happy to have me home at the computer. I am especially grateful to my editors and guides, Nana Twumasi and Kate Bradford, who believed in the vision of this book and pushed me to finish it.

Introduction

Pre-Algebra Out Loud, like the other books in the Out Loud series, is based on the premise that students will perform better in mathematics if they learn to read mathematical content more efficiently, pinpoint and study the important content with better retention, and write well in several different formats about mathematical concepts.

Too often, students learn about mathematics only from watching the teacher do problems and repeating these examples. These activities are considered tried-and-true learning strategies, but if we want students to think deeply or to challenge themselves to truly get it, we must ask them to read, interpret (think), and write about the content in their own words.

Meant for use as a supplemental resource, *Pre-Algebra Out Loud* provides several successful classroom-tested reading and writing strategies and activities that can be used to help students learn math at a deep level. Some of these activities ask students to paraphrase math text, create word maps, and build and use graphic organizers and tables. Other reading and writing to learn pre-algebra activities include the creation of written problems, a math glossary, and biographies of mathematicians. The activities are meant to teach students how to read, think, and write mathematics efficiently, effectively, and accurately.

The following eight chapters focus on the main pre-algebra topics: the basic tools of algebra; exploring infinite sets; topics in integers; number theory; fractions, decimals, and percents; equations and inequalities; visualizing algebra by graphing; and geometry. Each chapter contains two mini-lessons, as well as activities and reproducible worksheets that you can copy and use in your classroom. All reading and writing activities and strategies have been classroom tested with successful results.

The topics and activities are aligned with the new Common Core State Standards (CCSS) Initiative, a concrete description of standard practice for teaching K–12 mathematics. This is "a state-led effort coordinated by the National Governors Association Center for Best Practices (NGA Center) and the Council of Chief State School Officers (CCSSO). The standards were developed in collaboration with teachers, school administrators, and experts, to provide a clear and consistent framework to prepare our children for college and the workforce" (Common Core Initiative, 2011). This practical and necessary initiative:

1. Make[s] sense of problems and persevere[s] in solving them.
2. Reason[s] abstractly and quantitatively.
3. Construct[s] viable arguments and critique[s] the reasoning of others.
4. Model[s] with mathematics.
5. Use[s] appropriate tools strategically.
6. Attend[s] to precision (know when and how to give exact answers).
7. Look[s] for and make[s] use of structure.
8. Look[s] for and express[es] regularity in repeated reasoning [Common Core Initiative, 2011].

These eight standards form the basic practice of mathematics. Tables I.1 to I.3 give the appropriate standards from the CCSS for the curriculum in grades 6 through 8 that is addressed in each chapter of this book. Since *Pre-Algebra Out Loud* is not meant to be a comprehensive textbook, only the CCSS standards that target the mini-lessons in each chapter are given. Most of the current pre-algebra textbooks explore the curriculum that meets all of the CCSS standards.

Because *Pre-Algebra Out Loud* is to be used to enhance your students' exploration of algebra, all of the lessons and activities that follow can be adjusted to fit your individual instructional needs in your sixth-, seventh-, or eighth-grade classroom.

Table 1.1 Common Core Standards for Grade 6.

Grade 6 Objectives	Chapters and Mini-Lessons
6.RP: Ratios and proportional relationships	
Understand ratio concepts and use ratio reasoning to solve problems.	Mini-lesson 7.1
6.NS: Number System	
Compute fluently with multi-digit numbers and find common factors and multiples.	Chapter Six; Mini-lessons 4.1, 5.2, 6.1, and 6.2
Apply and extend previous understandings of numbers to the system of rational numbers.	Mini-lessons 5.1 and 7.2
6.EE: Expressions and equations	
Apply and extend previous understandings of arithmetic to algebraic expressions.	Mini-lessons 1.1 and 2.2
Reason about and solve one-variable equations and inequalities.	Chapter Two; Mini-lesson 1.2
Solve real-world and mathematical problems involving area, surface area, and volume.	Chapter Eight

Table 1.2 Common Core Standards for Grade 7.

Grade 7 Objectives	Chapters and Mini-Lessons
7.EE: Expressions and equations	
Use properties of operations to generate equivalent expressions.	Chapter One; Mini-lesson 5.2
Solve real-life and mathematical problems using numerical and algebraic expressions and equations.	Mini-lesson 2.1
7.G: Geometry	
Draw, construct, and describe geometrical figures and describe the relationship between them.	Chapter Seven; Mini-lessons 8.1 and 8.2

Table 1.3 Common Core Standards for Grade 8.

Grade 8 Objectives	Chapters and Mini-Lessons
8.EE: Expressions and equations	
Work with radicals and integer exponents.	Chapter Four; Mini-lesson 4.2
Understand the connections between proportional relationships, lines, and linear equations.	Chapter Three; Mini-lessons 3.1 and 3.2

PRE-ALGEBRA OUT LOUD

$$2x - 5x + 6x = 3x \quad y = mx + b$$

The Basic Tools of Algebra

WHAT? Introduction

When middle school students begin a pre-algebra course, they are introduced to a magnificent new world of mathematical symbols and concepts. By this time, they have learned the basic operations of arithmetic: addition, subtraction, multiplication, and division. They still need to continue practicing these skills along with learning higher-order skills. After becoming familiar with the newness of algebra, students are able to incorporate the new with the old to solve more complex problems. This chapter has two mini-lessons: one focusing on the basic symbols and concepts of algebra and the other on solving a simple equation. The first lesson, which introduces pre-algebra students to the basics and general concepts of algebra, lays the foundation for the activities for reading and writing to learn pre-algebra. It may be used as content for any of the activities that follow.

WHY? Objectives

By doing the activities in this chapter, pre-algebra students will:

- Find the major mathematical topics in the lessons that follow and in any pre-algebra text and write them out for use in future activities

- Create a math glossary demonstrating their understanding of the concepts of algebra

- Use semantic word maps to show the relationship between certain algebraic concepts

- Construct and use a concept circle to focus on a large algebraic idea and its components, rules, and examples

- Use algebraic terms creatively, allowing them to learn, understand, and apply these terms in a short story

- Examine, write out, and explain each step in the process of an algebraic algorithm or method of operation

Mini-Lesson 1.1 The Big Ideas of Algebra

CCSS Standard 6.EE: Expressions and Equations

Apply and extend previous understanding of arithmetic expressions.

A toolbox full of all the basic tools of algebra certainly contains a definition of *algebra*: a generalization of arithmetic in which symbols or letters called variables represent numbers and to which many of the same arithmetic properties and operations apply. This definition encompasses some of the major algebraic concepts and tools. Adding the following definitions to our toolbox yields plenty of tools to help learn about algebra:

- A *variable* is a symbol that stands for a number or a range of numbers.

- The letters X or Y can represent any number, so they are variables.

- A *constant* is a fixed number. For example, in $2x + 8$, the 8 is the constant.

- A *coefficient* is the multiplier next to a variable. For example, in $5x$ or $10a^2b$, the 5 and 10 are coefficients.

- The *arithmetic operations* are addition, subtraction, multiplication, and division: $+, -, \times, \div$.

- A *term* is a variable or variables with a coefficient or a constant. For example, in $4x + 6y - 8$, $4x$, $6y$ and -8 are terms.

- An *algebraic expression* is a mathematical phrase that can contain numbers, operators (add, subtract, multiply, divide), and at least one variable (like x or y.) For example, $4x + 6y - 8$ and $24ab - 3a^2b$ are algebraic expressions

- *Like terms* are terms that have the same variable (raised to the same power) but may have different coefficients. For example, $2x$, $5x$, and $6x$ are like terms.

When you introduce an exponential expression, such as x^2, show students the comparison of x with x^2. For example, if $x = 3$, then $x^2 = 9$. This reinforces the idea that x and x^2 are two different variables and therefore not *like terms*.

The following example describes many of these concepts:

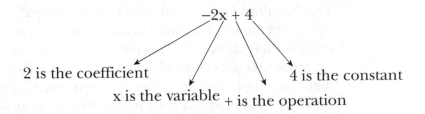

$$-2x + 4$$

2 is the coefficient

x is the variable + is the operation

4 is the constant

$-2x$ and 4 are *terms*. $-2x + 4$ is an *algebraic expression*.

These are useful tools for performing arithmetic operations.

Combining Like Terms

Completing an arithmetic operation on an algebraic expression requires collecting and combining like terms. Like terms can be thought of as similar things, like apples. For example, we can add the two like terms 4a and 5a by thinking of adding 5 apples to 4 apples to get 9 apples:

$$4a + 5a = 9a$$

Note that 20ab and 36ab are like terms, but 15a and 23ab are not like terms. The variables a and ab are not the same variables. Similarly, $5x^2$ and $7x^2$ are like terms, but $5x^2$ and $7x^3$ are not like terms and cannot be combined.

Here are some other examples of combining like terms:

Example 1: $5x - 2x + 3y + 6y = 3x + 9y$. The 5x and 2x can be combined and the 3y and 6y can be combined because they are like terms, but since 3x and 9y are not like terms, the operation is completed when you get $3x + 9y$, which is in simplified form.

Example 2: $14a - 3 + 12a + 5 = 14a + 12a - 3 + 5 = 26a + 2$. Here we moved, or *commuted*, the like terms 14a and 12a so they sat next to each other and then combined them by adding the coefficients. This is because the operation addition has a property called the *commutative property*. We discuss this property in detail, along with other number properties, in mini-lesson 2.2 in Chapter Two.

Activity 1.1 The Writing Is on the Wall

$2x - 5x + 6x = 3x \quad A(B + C) = AB + AC \quad 4 \times 5 = 5 \times 4 \quad 2(3 + 5)^2 + (-1)^2 \quad y = mx + b$

WHAT? Description

Elementary teachers often use a word wall or bulletin board to help students learn the spelling and vocabulary of math terms. Your wall will be more useful to students if you group terms—for example, the Top Ten, Fabulous Five, or Foremost Four mathematics concepts—from each lesson or chapter. Students should be asked to give the key concepts and explain their choice of concepts.

Students collect significant pre-algebra or algebra concepts and terms that they then use to construct their math glossaries (described in activity 1.3) and add to their mathematical vocabulary.

WHY? Objectives

During this activity, pre-algebra students:

- Choose key concepts from a section in their textbook or that day's lesson
- Collect words to help construct a math glossary over the entire course

HOW? Example

The first two examples that follow come from two different lessons in a pre-algebra textbook. The first list gives what a student might consider the five most important terms from a lesson on linear equations—the "fabulous five." The second list gives the "top ten" concepts from a lesson on inequalities. The third example consists of what an algebra student might give as the seven most "sensational symbols" from the entire study of algebra.

Fabulous Five Terms from a Lesson on Linear Equations

variable

coefficient

constant

like terms

solution

Top Ten Concepts from a Lesson on Inequalities

inequality	interval solution
less than sign	interval notation
greater than sign	number line graph
less than or equal to	positive or negative infinity
greater than or equal to	compound inequality

Seven Sensational Symbols from Algebra

$=$	$\pm$	$\neq$	;
$\emptyset$	$\geq$	$\times$	

Worksheet 1.1 The Writing Is on the Wall

NAME _____ DATE _____

$2x - 5x + 6x = 3x$ $A(B + C) = AB + AC$ $4 \times 5 = 5 \times 4$ $2(3 + 5)^2 + (-1)^2$ $y = mx + b$

Directions: Choose five concepts that are key to algebra. Look for terms that are related in the same way to these concepts. You may use today's lesson or a chapter from your pre-algebra textbook. Then try finding six symbols that are commonly used in algebra and list them under the Sensational Six Symbols. Be creative!

Fabulous Five Terms from a Lesson on Algebraic Expressions

Six Sensational Symbols from the Basics of Algebra

Activity 1.2 Semantic Word Maps

$2x - 5x + 6x = 3x$ $A(B + C) = AB + AC$ $4 \times 5 = 5 \times 4$ $2(3 + 5)^2 + (-1)^2$ $y = mx + b$

WHAT? Description

Semantic word maps depict and display the relationships between key concepts and terms. These word maps often resemble flowcharts or webs connecting mathematical terms. Arrows connect related concepts and often display a hierarchy of the terms, where one term is a set and the others are subsets of that set. For example, if algebra is the main set, then equations, variables, and constants are all parts of the set or subsets of the set "algebra."

After students have completed their semantic word maps, you might pose critical-thinking questions—questions that go beyond the lesson—that encourage students to think of the relationships between the subsets—for example: If equations and variables are both subsets of algebra, is a variable a subset of an equation?

WHY? Objectives

During this activity, pre-algebra students:

- Explore relationships between mathematical concepts and terms
- See the hierarchy of key concepts
- Create study guides displaying key concepts

HOW? Example

Consider the related algebraic concepts in the map shown on page 8. Place the terms in the word map showing their relationship to each other. Add arrows and circles as needed. *Hint:* Look for the larger set (equations) and decide which of the concepts are parts of this set. There may be more than one set and some concepts (subsets) may be parts of more than one set. Peruse the terms, looking for one word or concept that is made from the other words or parts. Clearly, an equation is formed from the other terms, like variables or constants, expression, term, variable, coefficient, constant, and the equal sign.

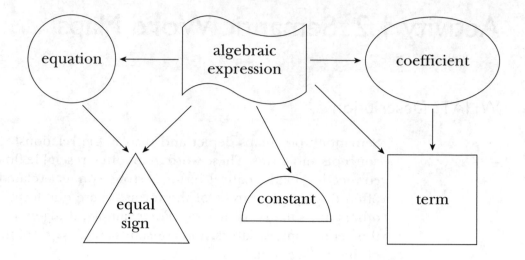

Worksheet 1.2 Semantic Word Maps

NAME _____   DATE _____

$2x - 5x + 6x = 3x$ $A(B + C) = AB + AC$ $4 \times 5 = 5 \times 4$ $2(3 + 5)^2 + (-1)^2$ $y = mx + b$

Consider the following terms related to algebra:

operations   variables
problems   quality sign
solutions   combining like terms

You may want to group some of these terms together before you start.

Place one term in each figure in the diagram, and draw arrows showing how these terms might be related to each other. There is more than one way to fill in the shapes. Be prepared to share and perhaps defend your choices that make up your semantic map.

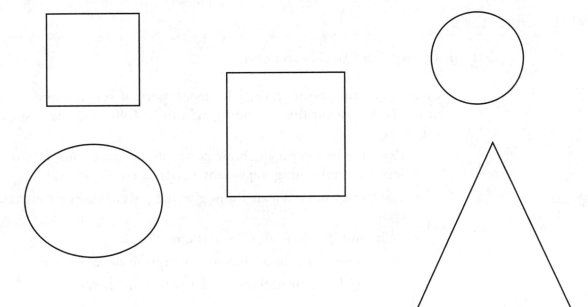

The Basic Tools of Algebra

Activity 1.3 Math Glossary

$$2x - 5x + 6x = 3x \quad A(B + C) = AB + AC \quad 4 \times 5 = 5 \times 4 \quad 2(3 + 5)^2 + (-1)^2 \quad y = mx + b$$

WHAT? Description

Asking students to collect the important words or concepts from a chapter or section of text is one of the first steps in building mathematical literacy. Whether by handwriting in their math notebooks or using computer word processing or spreadsheet programs, students can input the terms from each chapter so that by the end of this course, they will have created a dictionary or glossary they can use during quizzes or in future courses.

It is important to give students a format for displaying the terms. For example, a student might be asked to give each term's part of speech: a noun, verb, adjective, and so on. Then the students might be asked to give a definition from the reading or class notes and a definition or description of their own. See the suggested format in worksheet 1.3.

WHY? Objectives

In this activity, pre-algebra students:

- Create a math glossary giving the term, part of speech, and definition of a concept they are studying and by following these steps (objectives):
    - Read the lesson on algebraic concepts, and take notes on the lesson, highlighting important words or concepts.
    - List the significant terms, and give the part of speech for each term.
    - Write out the definition from the textbook.
    - Write a personal definition or description of each term.
    - Write a phrase or statement using the word correctly.

HOW? Example

These are a few terms that could be used in the glossary:

algebra	variable	constant
algebraic expression	algebraic equation	coefficient

Worksheet 1.3 Math Glossary

NAME _____   DATE _____

$$2x - 5x + 6x = 3x \quad A(B + C) = AB + AC \quad 4 \times 5 = 5 \times 4 \quad 2(3 + 5)^2 + (-1)^2 \quad y = mx + b$$

Directions: Reread the first lesson on algebra before you begin a math glossary. Choose at least five concepts or words, and fill in the matrix below. The first one is filled in for you.

Word or Concept	Part of Speech	Text Definition	My Definition	Example Phrase
Variable	Noun	Symbol or letter that stands for a numerical value or values	A letter like x or y that you can replace with a number	The variable in the equation x + 3 = 5 is x and stands for the number 2.

Activity 1.4 Concept Circles

WHAT? Description

The creation or use of concept circles is one of the more versatile reading and post-reading activities (Vacca & Vacca, 1999). A concept circle usually focuses on a single concept and its important features. Features, or descriptors of the concept, are placed within sectors of the circle. The circle is generally divided into quarters; however, more sectors may be used if needed. Though the concept circle is traditionally a circle, it could also be diagrammed in a square or any two-dimensional figure.

Concept circles may be teacher created and used to quiz students:

- Given the descriptors contained in the sections of the circle, students identify the concept.
- Given the concept and descriptors, students select which of the descriptors is incorrect.
- Given the concept and a few descriptors, students fill in the rest of the circle.
- Concept circles may also be student created:
  - The teacher gives the concept, and students fill in the sections of the circle.
  - The student selects the concept from the reading and fills in the sections of the circle.

WHY? Objectives

During this activity, pre-algebra students:

- Categorize information from the reading
- Review features and descriptors of a certain concept
- Self-assess their reading comprehension

Example of a Concept Circle for an Algebraic Expression

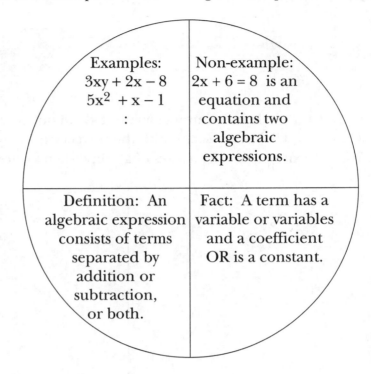

In this example, the circle is divided into four sectors. However, you may divide the concept circle into as many sectors needed. Each sector gives information that helps form a word picture of what an algebraic expression is, and the sectors may include any of the following: definition, description, examples, nonexamples, uses, facts, or features. A few of these categories are explained below.

- *Nonexamples* are examples that are related to the concept but are not examples of it. The nonexample for an algebraic expression in the concept circle here is the equation $2x + 6 = 8$, which is actually two algebraic expressions divided by the equals sign, giving an equation.

- *Uses* may include where the concept is used in mathematics, other courses, or in the physical world.

- *Facts* might be rules or theorems that make up or apply to the concept.

- *Features* are parts or attributes of the given concept. Other descriptors or components of the concept may be used. Examples include numerical expressions, pictures, symbols, or words that depict the concept.

Worksheet 1.4 Concept Circle Activity: Algebra

NAME _____   DATE _____

$2x - 5x + 6x = 3x$ $A(B + C) = AB + AC$ $4 \times 5 = 5 \times 4$ $2(3 + 5)^2 + (-1)^2$ $y = mx + b$

Directions: Divide the circle into four sectors using definition, example, nonexample, and uses for each sector. Fill in each sector with the correct explanation according to its category. We will share our word pictures of algebra when we are all finished.

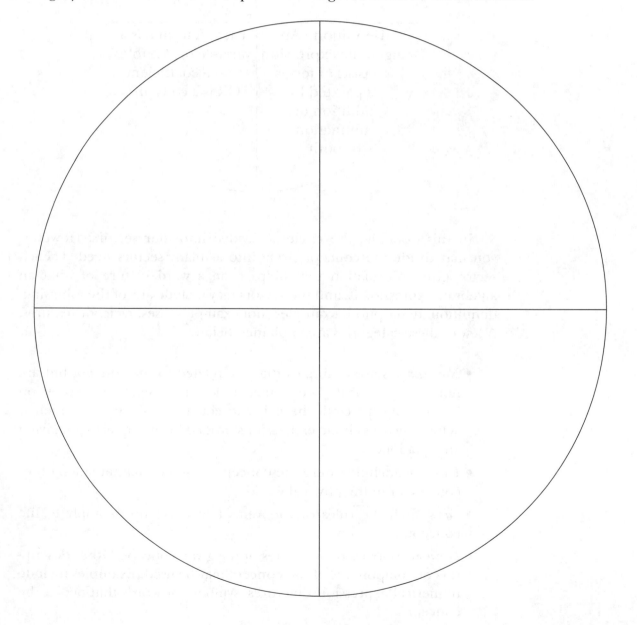

Pre-Algebra Out Loud

Worksheet 1.5 Concept Circle Activity: Combining Like Terms

NAME _____   DATE _____

$2x - 5x + 6x = 3x$ $A(B + C) = AB + AC$ $4 \times 5 = 5 \times 4$ $2(3 + 5)^2 + (-1)^2$ $y = mx + b$

Directions: Decide on how many categories/sectors to divide the circle into and give their titles. Then fill in each sector using the correct explanation according to its category. We will share our word pictures of combining like terms when we are all finished.

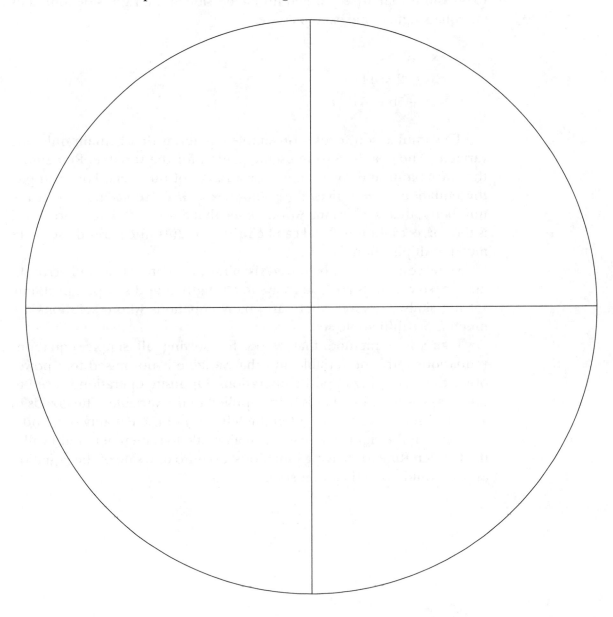

The Basic Tools of Algebra

CCSS Standard 6.EE: Expressions and Equations

Reason about and solve one-variable equations and inequalities.

This mini-lesson introduces problem-solving techniques to pre-algebra students. Algebra is all about problem solving, and a vital tool for mathematical problem solving is the equation. An equation consists of an algebraic expression set equal to another algebraic expression, one of which may be a constant.

An *equation* is a statement asserting the equality of two algebraic expressions that are separated into a left side and a right side joined by an equals sign. Some examples are:

$$x = 9$$
$$3x + 2 = 11$$
$$4a + 5b = 6a - 8$$

This mini-lesson focuses on simple equations that contain only one variable. The goal is to solve each equation for the variable. Remember that variables stand for numbers or a range of numbers. For example, the equation $2x = 8$ gives the solution $x = 4$. By replacing x with the number 4, that is, checking work, we see that $2 \times 4 = 8$. Therefore $x = 4$ is the correct solution. 2×4 can be written as $2(4)$; the parentheses here mean multiplication.

Many equations can be solved visually or by mental trial and error. In fact, these methods are good ways to strengthen and sharpen problem-solving skills. However, there are many equations whose solutions are much more difficult to see.

There is a method that works for solving all simple equations (equations with one variable and that variable is not raised to a power other than 1): using opposite operations. Opposite operation is used to undo every operation that is being applied to the variable. The goal is to get x by itself on one side (often the left side) of the equality sign and a constant on the right. There is one major rule to remember, and I call it the Golden Rule for Solving Equations: do unto one side of the equation as you would do to the other side.

Doing the same thing to both sides of the equation yields an equivalent equation, an equation with the same solution. For example,

$x - 9 = 12$	The opposite of subtracting 9 is adding 9.
$x - 9 + 9 = 12 + 9$	Add 9 to both sides and simplify.
$x = 21$	Checking the solution: replacing x with 21 gives $21 - 9 = 12$ which is true.

Always check your answer!

 ## Teaching Tip

When demonstrating how to solve an equation with more than one or two steps, show all of the work. Students get frustrated when they do not understand how to get from one equation to the next equivalent equation. Only after much practice will they understand when two opposite operations can be completed in one step when solving an equation.

Activity 1.5 Math Story

$$2x - 5x + 6x = 3x \quad A(B + C) = AB + AC \quad 4 \times 5 = 5 \times 4 \quad 2(3 + 5)^2 + (-1)^2 \quad y = mx + b$$

WHAT? Description

For this activity, give students a list of terms or concepts specific to algebra and ask them to use all of the terms correctly to write a short story. This activity may be used during or after the lesson containing the specified terms. Asking students to use this language requires that they learn the meaning of these terms.

Encourage the student writers to be creative, but also to pay close attention to the meanings of the terms they use. The stories may be fiction or nonfiction. They may be witty, silly, sad, or dramatic. However, give some guidelines for them to follow when creating their stories (see the assignment criteria on worksheet 1.6). Being explicit about what constitutes an A paper is equally important to the student writer and the teacher reader/grader.

WHY? Objectives

During this activity, pre-algebra students will:

- Write a short story using the given algebraic terms
- Use a dictionary or algebra text to find definitions of unknown words
- Practice using and writing about math terms correctly

HOW? Example

For this example, the terms are *solve, equal, terms, equation,* and *problem*.

This is a silly short story about problem solving:

> Ex had a problem he needed to solve involving dividing a solution into two equal parts. So he approached Wy for help. Together they composed an equation, setting the term 2x equal to 10 cups. Ex said, "We must state that x = amount of cups of the solution when divided into 2 parts." Solving the equation seemed very simple: find the amount of one of the parts. Ex and Wy brainstormed and found 5 was the solution. Ex and Wy decided they work well together.
>
> The moral to the story is this: if Ex doesn't give you the answer, try Wy!

Worksheet 1.6 Math Story Activity

NAME _____ DATE _____

$$2x - 5x + 6x = 3x \quad A(B + C) = AB + AC \quad 4 \times 5 = 5 \times 4 \quad 2(3 + 5)^2 + (-1)^2 \quad y = mx + b$$

Directions: Use terms from the following list to write a short story:

- Variable
- Constant
- Coefficient
- Algebraic expression

- Term
- Like terms
- Combining like terms
- Equation

- Solution
- Problem solving
- Opposite operation
- Equivalent

Assignment Criteria

1. Use at least 9 of the 12 listed terms in your story.
2. Use each term correctly. Use the text or dictionary to check on definitions and correct use of terms. You may be creative with each term; but in at least one place, use the term correctly or in a manner that clearly demonstrates you understand what the term means.
3. Your story may be fiction or nonfiction.
4. Your story should contain an introduction and a conclusion and follow a logical story line.
5. Your story should be at least one page but no more than two pages. You may begin your story on the line below.

_____

_____

_____

_____

_____

_____

_____

Activity 1.6 Algorithm Writing

$$2x - 5x + 6x = 3x \quad A(B + C) = AB + AC \quad 4 \times 5 = 5 \times 4 \quad 2(3 + 5)^2 + (-1)^2 \quad y = mx + b$$

WHAT? Description

An *algorithm* is a step-by-step, computational problem-solving procedure with a finite number of steps. During the algorithm writing activity, students are asked to take a computational procedure or equation and write out the problem-solving process in words. This activity helps demystify algebraic problem solving by allowing students to explain each step of the process integrating their own language with the appropriate algebraic terms and concepts. The math glossary is useful for this activity.

This activity is also an excellent way to address students' use or misuse of math terms. Although algorithms are the "how to do it" part of problem solving, this activity helps students to see why each step works. Asking a student to explain a process to another student who does not know how to do it or is struggling to understand should encourage the writer/explainer to explain in more detail or to consider questions students might have.

WHY? Objectives

During this activity, pre-algebra students will:

- Focus on the steps used to solve an algebraic equation
- Practice writing and communicating mathematics to a certain audience
- Learn how to use and write mathematical terms correctly

HOW? Example

Here's an example of a pre-algebra student's algorithm writing and how it could be improved.

Solve the following algebraic equation and write out each step as you complete it using both the appropriate algebraic terms and your own words. Imagine that you are explaining the problem-solving process to a student who has not yet mastered the process.

Problem:	$8x-3(x+4)=18$
$8x - 3x - 12 = 18$	I first multiplied the -3 by the two terms $(x + 4)$. Watch the negative sign.
$5x - 12 = 18$	Then I combined like terms and subtracted 8x minus 3x, which is 5x.
$5x - 12 + 12 = 18 + 12$	I added 12 to both sides because of opposite operations.*
$5x = 30$	I did the adding.
$\dfrac{5x}{5} = \dfrac{30}{5}$	I divided both sides by 5.
$x = 6$	I got the answer x = 6. I checked it to make sure it worked!

Although this student offered adequate explanations, I would encourage her to write "I distributed" instead of "I first multiplied," and "I simplified" rather than "I did the adding." The asterisk indicates that the teacher asked the student to explain what she meant by "because of opposite operations." However, that phrase shows that the student writer understood why she must add 12 to both sides of the equation.

Worksheet 1.7 Algorithm Writing

NAME _____   DATE _____

$2x - 5x + 6x = 3x \quad A(B + C) = AB + AC \quad 4 \times 5 = 5 \times 4 \quad 2(3 + 5)^2 + (-1)^2 \quad y = mx + b$

Directions: Solve the following algebraic equation, and write out each step as you complete it using both the appropriate algebraic terms and your own words. Imagine that you are explaining the problem-solving process to a student who has not yet mastered the process.

Write each step in the left column. Then for each step, explain in detail what you did and why you did it in the corresponding cell in the right column. Be careful not to leave any steps out!

Problem: $20x - 6 + 5x = 15x - 14$

Problem-Solving Steps: How It Works	Explanation for Each Step: Why It Works

Activity 1.7 One-Minute Summary

$2x - 5x + 6x = 3x$ $A(B + C) = AB + AC$ $4 \times 5 = 5 \times 4$ $2(3 + 5)^2 + (-1)^2$ $y = mx + b$

WHAT? Description

The one-minute summary or one-minute essay is a familiar assignment to many teachers in other disciplines. This brief writing activity yields a wealth of information to both writer and reader.

Ask students to free-write (write without worrying about grammar, punctuation, or spelling errors) on a particular topic for one minute. These summaries may be used at the beginning, middle, or end of the course or unit or more than once during a lesson or over the semester, providing students with a quick assessment of their grasp of a topic. One-minute summaries can also be handed in to assess how well each student knows the topic and see how much they have learned. They need not be graded.

Begin this activity by saying to the students: "Take out a sheet of paper. We are going to free-write for exactly one minute on one topic, which I will give you. Free-writing means to write down everything that comes to mind about the topic, whether it be definition, shapes, examples, words associated with our word, or any other related terms that come to mind, without worrying about spelling or grammar rules. Just write everything you know or remember about the topic without stopping as you write. In exactly one minute, I will say, 'Stop,' and you must stop writing. When you are finished, we will share our writings with each other. Then you will hand these in, and at the end of the unit we will repeat this activity. I will hand back your original one-minute summary and you will see how much you have learned."

One-minute summary works better if you choose terms with a narrower scope. For example, *pre-algebra* is too broad; however, *integers* would be a very good concept for a one-minute summary.

WHY? Objectives

During the one-minute summary, pre-algebra students:

- Free-associate or free-write about an algebraic topic in a limited amount of time
- Self-assess their comprehension of a lesson or a concept
- Demonstrate their comprehension of concepts to their teachers

HOW? Example

Here are some sample algebra topics:

Linear equation	xy plane
Cartesian coordinate system	Line
x and y intercepts	Ordered pairs
Slope	

Example of a one-minute summary: "A linear equation has a variable like x, and it has an equal sign and some other numbers called constants and coefficients. It has only one answer all the time unless it has two variables x and y. Then it is a line with all the points on the line as solutions for x and y."

$$2x - 5x + 6x = 3x \quad y = mx + b$$

Exploring Infinite Sets

WHAT? Introduction

Usually mathematics courses begin with an exploration of the set of numbers that will be addressed or used in that course. The first lesson in this chapter focuses on defining and describing all of the large sets of numbers commonly used in algebra, followed by reading and writing activities that enhance students' understanding of these sets. Mini-lesson 2.2 discusses the properties of the set of real numbers, the largest set of numbers explored in pre-algebra curricula.

WHY? Objectives

Using the activities in this chapter, pre-algebra students will:

- Complete a matching exercise in a magic square format to illustrate the comparison and contrast of certain infinite sets
- Write one-minute summaries for self-assessment
- Work with peers to create graphic organizers to demonstrate the hierarchy or set or subset relationship of infinite sets
- Read, write, and use mathematical symbols in place of words (activity 2.4)

- Create a mathematics glossary using the major terms related to infinite sets of numbers

- Complete a semantic feature analysis (activity 2.7) showing different ways of expressing sets

- Paraphrase text and share their writings with other students

Mini-Lesson 2.1   Infinite Sets

CCSS Standard 6.NS: Number System

Apply and extend previous understandings of numbers to the system of rational numbers.

A *set* is a collection of elements or objects. An *infinite set* is a nonterminating list of numbers; it does not end, and it follows a prescribed number pattern. Brackets are used to denote sets.

We will consider the objects to be numbers in this book. For example, in the set of natural numbers |N ... "N" can be expressed as a roster or list contained inside the braces:

$$|N = \{1, 2, 3, 4, \ldots\}$$

The ellipses "..." mean the list of numbers continues in that pattern forever.

The set of whole numbers is the set of natural numbers along with the number 0:

$$|W = \{0, 1, 2, 3, 4, \ldots\}$$

The numbers in ||N and ||W are infinite, meaning they go on forever. In fact, for any large natural number, we can find another number by adding 1 to that number.

Another important infinite set is the set of integers (|I):

$$|I = \{\ldots -3, -2, -1, 0, 1, 2, 3, \ldots\}.$$

Note that the integers contain no ending or beginning number. In fact we denote the smallest negative integer with an abstract expression:

$-\infty$ (read "negative infinity")

and the greatest integer as

$+\infty$ (read "positive infinity").

Some infinite sets are difficult to express as lists. For example, the set of rational numbers (which is actually the set of fractions or any number that can be written as a fraction) is infinite but cannot be expressed in a roster (which is just a list of numbers). What would the first number after 0 be in this: $\frac{1}{2}$? .1?, .01? .001? In fact any of these numbers could be considered in the middle of the set! Try to imagine the smallest fraction or the largest fraction.

Yet the set of fractions can be expressed in what is called *set-builder notation.* The set of rational numbers is abbreviated as |Q and is defined as this set:

$$|\mathbb{Q} = \{x|x =, a/b, \text{ where a and b are integers, but } b \neq 0\}.$$

This is read, "The set of all x such that x = a **divided by** b, where a and b are integers but b cannot be equal to 0."

We cannot divide any number or expression by 0.

The largest infinite set that we will work with in the pre-algebra course is the set of real numbers, often referred to as the *reals,* expressed like this: |R. The real numbers are the numbers that we see and use in the real world, such as counting numbers, integers, fractions, and decimals.

One way to understand and visualize the reals is to think of a horizontal number line that goes on infinitely in the positive direction and infinitely in the negative direction. All the points on the number line have a number value that gives the distance from 0; the sign (positive or negative) determines the direction the value is from 0. Numbers with no sign are considered positive. All values that lie on this number line, including fractions that are not labeled on the number line below, are real numbers:

```
 -5   -4   -3   -2   -1    0    1    2    3    4    5    6
```

Real Number Line

Below are some examples of real numbers. Many of them are familiar. Students will see a few of them as they move on in their study of algebra.

$$4, .5, 1/2, \frac{-5}{7}, 0, \frac{\sqrt{2}}{2}, \pi, \sqrt{6}, \pi^2$$

☀ Teaching Tip

It is often difficult for students to grasp what the infinity sign (∞) means. It is thought to be a number, but it is not. It is an abstract concept that means the numbers are getting very large ($+\infty$) or very small ($-\infty$) and are endless.

Activity 2.1 Magic Square

WHAT? Description

The magic square activity combines a matching activity with mathematics and a puzzle of a magic square (Vacca & Vacca, 1999). The format of the matching activity consists of two columns, one for concepts and one for definitions, facts, examples, or descriptions. In solving the matching activity, the student places the numbers in the corresponding lettered squares inside the magic square.

A	B	C
D	E	F
G	H	I

To check their answers, students add the numbers in each row, in each column, and in each diagonal. These sums should be equal. This sum is referred to as the square's "magic number." Sometimes only the numbers in the rows will sum up to the magic number and one or more diagonal contain values that do not add up to the magic number.

WHY? Objectives

During this activity, pre-algebra students:

- Learn the concept of infinite sets
- See the mix of interest and mystery of the mathematics of infinite sets
- Learn about the concept and properties of magic squares

The magic squares below are 3-by-3 unit squares. Notice that the cells in these particular magic squares contain all whole numbers from 1 to 9 with no repeats. When you add the numbers in each column, in each row, and in each diagonal, your sum is 15. This number is called the *magic number*.

Not all magic squares have consecutive numbers in its cells. However, all the numbers in each row and in each column must add up to the same (magic) number. There are some magic squares in which the diagonal numbers do not sum up to the same number. Clearly, magic squares must have the same number of rows or columns; thus, they are squares.

The activities in this chapter show some ways to integrate the use of magic squares with algebra. The first three magic squares below contain the numbers 1 through 9, but they in different cells. These 3-by-3 squares are very special and used often to build other different magic squares.

8	1	6
3	5	7
4	9	2

6	1	8
7	5	3
2	9	4

4	9	2
3	5	7
8	1	6

Worksheet 2.1 Building a Magic Square Activity

NAME _____ DATE _____

Directions: This magic square has the magic number of 39. *Note:* The diagonal sums do not necessarily yield the same sum as rows and columns in this example.

2	7	18	12
8	5	11	15
13	17	6	3
16	10	4	9

Use the same numbers shown in the above magic square to construct a different magic square. Does it have the same magic number?

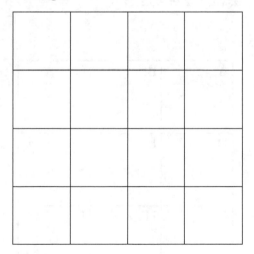

Magic number =

Worksheet 2.2 Magic Square Activity for Infinite Sets

NAME _____   DATE _____

$2x - 5x + 6x = 3x$ $A(B + C) = AB + AC$ $4 \times 5 = 5 \times 4$ $2(3 + 5)^2 + (-1)^2$ $y = mx + b$

Directions: Select the best answer for each of the terms on the left from the numbered descriptors or facts on the right. Put the number in the proper lettered cell in the magic square. Add each row and each column. If these sums are the same number, then you have found the magic number and matched the correct terms with their descriptors or rules. You may need to use your text and notes to match the correct sets with their descriptors or rules.

Terms	**Descriptors, Rules**
A. Reals	1. $\{ \ldots -3, -2, -1, 0, 1, 2, 3, \ldots \}$
B. Integers	2. Can be expressed as an improper fraction
C. Natural numbers	3. All rational numbers can be expressed in this form
D. Rational numbers	4. { }
E. Irrational numbers	5. {x|x is not a rational number}
F. Fractions	6. All numbers that lie on a number line
G. Mixed number	7. Fractions with integers for numerators and denominators
H. Wholes	8. The set of whole numbers without 0
I. Empty set	9. $\{0, 1, 2, 3, 4, \ldots\}$

A	B	C
D	E	F
G	H	I

Magic number =

Activity 2.2 One-Minute Summary

$2x - 5x + 6x = 3x$ $A(B + C) = AB + AC$ $4 \times 5 = 5 \times 4$ $2(3 + 5)^2 + (-1)^2$ $y = mx + b$

WHAT? Description

The one-minute summary or one-minute essay is a familiar assignment to many teachers in other disciplines. This brief writing activity yields a wealth of information to writer and reader.

Ask students to free-write (write without worrying about grammar, punctuation, or spelling errors) on a particular topic for one minute. One-minute summaries may be used at the beginning, middle, or end of the course or unit or more than once during a lesson or over the semester, providing students with a quick assessment of their grasp of a topic. One-minute summaries can also be handed in to assess how well each student knows the topic and see how much they have learned. They need not be graded.

Begin this activity by saying to the students, "Take out a sheet of paper. We are going to free-write for exactly one minute on one topic, which I will give you soon. Free-writing means writing down everything that comes to mind about the topic, whether it be definition, shapes, examples, words associated with our word, or any other related terms that come to mind, without worrying about spelling or grammar rules. Just write everything you know or remember about the topic without stopping as you write. In exactly one minute, I will say, 'Stop,' and you must stop writing. When you are finished, we will share our writings with each other. Then you will hand these in, and at the end of the unit we will repeat this activity. I will hand back your original one-minute summary, and you will see how much you have learned."

One-minute summary works best if you choose terms with a narrower scope. For example, *pre-algebra* is too broad; however, *integers* would be a very good concept for a one-minute summary.

WHY? Objectives

During this activity, pre-algebra students:

- Free-associate and free-write about a particular mathematical topic in a limited amount of time
- Self-assess their comprehension of a concept or lesson without worrying about grammar or spelling and grades
- Demonstrate their comprehension of topics to the teacher

HOW? Examples

Prompts

- "Take out a clean sheet of paper. We are going to free-write for exactly one minute on one topic. To free-write means to write continuously without worrying about grammar rules or correct spelling. Just write everything you think or know about the following topic, without picking up your pencil."

- "We are going to write one-minute summaries on certain topics. Use the back of your homework and free-write, meaning write everything you know about the set of reals. Do not worry about spelling or grammar. When I say 'Go,' you will start, and you will stop when I stay 'Stop!'"

Sample Topics

- Real numbers
- Infinite sets
- Properties of the reals
- Distributive

Here are some examples of students' one-minute summaries of infinite sets. The summaries are in quotation marks and teacher comments in brackets:

- "Infinite sets go on and on and on forever, like the set of counting numbers 1,2,3,4, ... Every time you say a number, I can give one bigger." [Very good! Is there a smallest counting number? Yes, it is 1.]

- "Infinite is like outer space. You can keep going and going, and then there is still more to go. I guess that's why sets of numbers are infinite 'cause they keep on going." [Good. Is there an infinite number of pieces of sand on Earth?]

Mini-Lesson 2.2   Properties of the Real Numbers

CCSS Standard 7.EE: Expressions and Equations

Use properties of operations to generate equivalent expressions.

This lesson involves the set of real numbers and its properties. Understanding these properties gives students more tools to use when problem solving. All of the infinite sets of numbers we've explored in this chapter have certain properties dealing with the operations: addition, subtraction, multiplication, and division. Since the reals are the largest set of numbers used in pre-algebra, we first consider all the real number properties. Each property has a rule, a particular set of numbers, and one or more operations.

The following list sets out all of the properties students will use in pre-algebra and algebra, along with the rule and examples. Let a, b, and c stand for real numbers.

- The *commutative property* holds for the set of reals with addition and multiplication. *Hint: commute* means "move."

Rule	Example
$a + b = b + a$	$2 + 3 = 3 + 2$
$ab = ba$	$4 \times 5 = 5 \times 4$

In algebra, multiplication is written as "ab" or "2y"; that is, the multiplication symbol is not used. Therefore, the rule is ab = ba or 4(5) = 5(4). The parentheses here are used to denote multiplication.

- The *associative property* holds for the reals with addition and multiplication. *Hint: associate* means "pair up."

Rule	Example
$(a + b) + c = a + (b + c)$	$(2 + 4) + 6 = 2 + (4 + 6) = 12$
$(ab)c = a(bc)$	$[2(4)]6 = 2[4(6)] = 48$

When doing several operations, always do what is in the parentheses first.

- The *distributive property* holds for the reals with multiplication distributed over addition or subtraction. This is one of the most useful properties in algebra! *Hint: distribute* means "pair off."

Rule	Example
$a(b + c) = ab + ac$	$3(x + 2) = 3x + 3(2) = 3x + 6$
$a(b - c) = ab - ac$	$3(x - 2) = 3x - 3(2) = 3x - 6$

- The set of reals contains an *additive identity*: the number 0. This means that there exists a number (0) that, when added to any real number, gives that real number.

Rule	Example
$a + 0 = 0 + a = a$	$3 + 0 = 0 + 3 = 3$

- The set of reals contains a *multiplicative identity*: the number 1. This means that there exists a number (1) that when multiplied by a real number gives that number.

Rule	Example
$1(b) = b(1)$	$1(5) = 5(1)$

- Each real number has an *additive inverse*: it is the opposite of that number. The sum of each real number added to its opposite is equal to the additive identity 0.

Rule	Example
$a + (-a) = (-a) + a = 0$	$7 + (-7) = (-7) + 7 = 0$

- Every real number except 0 has a *multiplicative inverse,* which is called the *reciprocal* of each real number. The product of a real number and its multiplicative inverse gives the multiplicative identity 1. N: The real number 0 has no multiplicative inverse since $\frac{1}{0}$ does not exist. You cannot divide a nonzero number by zero.

Rule	Example
$b \cdot \frac{1}{b} = \frac{1}{b} \cdot b = 1$	$2(\frac{1}{2}) = \frac{1}{2}(2) = 1$

☀ Teaching Tip

Students often ask why it's impossible to divide by 0. One answer might be: "Consider 6 divided by 2. A number, 3, when multiplied by 2, gives 6, which gives our solution, 3. This is one definition of division. However, when 6 is divided by 0, there is no number that when multiplied by 0 gives 6."

In the following activities, students will consider which properties hold for which sets of numbers.

Worksheet 2.3 Magic Square Activity for Properties of Real Numbers

NAME _____   DATE _____

$2x - 5x + 6x = 3x$ $A(B + C) = AB + AC$ $4 \times 5 = 5 \times 4$ $2(3 + 5)^2 + (-1)^2$ $y = mx + b$

Directions: Select the best answer for each of the terms on the left from the numbered descriptors or facts on the right. Put the number in the proper square in the magic square below. Add each row, and then add each column. If these sums are the same number, you have found the magic number and matched the correct terms with their rules.

Concepts	Rules
A. Commutative for addition	10. $3 \times \frac{1}{3} = 1 = \frac{1}{3} \times 3$
B. Associative for multiplication	20. $3(a + 2) = 3a + 6$
C. Distributive for multiplication over addition	30. $2 + 0 = 2 = 0 + 2$
D. Additive identity	40. $5 + 6 = 6 + 5$
E. Additive inverse	50. $4 + (-4) = 0 = (-4) + 4$
F. Multiplicative identity	60. 1 over the number
G. Commutative for multiplication	70. $6 \times 1 = 6 = 1 \times 6$
H. Multiplicative inverse	80. $12 \times 10 = 10 \times 12$
I. Reciprocal	90. $(3 \times 4) \times 5 = 3 \times (4 \times 5)$

A	B	C
D	E	F
G	H	I

Magic number =

Activity 2.3 Graphic Organizers

WHAT? Description

Graphic organizers (Barron, 1969) are schematics created to show connections between key concepts, similar to the semantic word maps in Chapter One. A graphic organizer is a geometric figure that draws attention to key concepts. Graphic organizers can be used to display subsets (parts) of larger sets; for example: the set of integers is a subset of the set of real numbers. When completed, graphic organizers may be used as a study guide or as a part of a bulletin board.

Teachers and students can create graphic organizers for use during prereading, reading, or postreading of the lesson. Teachers might present a graphic organizer to the class as a prereading demonstration to elicit students' prior knowledge of the concepts to be studied. Working in groups, students might brainstorm terms related to some larger concept and create their own graphic organizers.

WHY? Objectives

During this activity, pre-algebra students will:

- Activate prior knowledge of concepts
- Make connections between key concepts
- Summarize and organize main ideas from the reading for reviewing purposes

HOW? Example

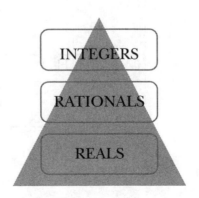

The graphic at the left is often referred to as a "pyramid," although it is actually a triangle because pyramids in geometry are three-dimensional solids. This graphic (triangle) can be used to demonstrate the relationships of infinite sets. Three infinite sets are placed on the pyramid, with the largest set, the reals, in the larger part or base of the triangle or pyramid. The rational numbers are part of the reals, and the integers are part of the rational numbers.

Worksheet 2.4 Graphic Organizers

NAME _____ DATE _____

$$2x - 5x + 6x = 3x \quad A(B + C) = AB + AC \quad 4 \times 5 = 5 \times 4 \quad 2(3 + 5)^2 + (-1)^2 \quad y = mx + b$$

Reals

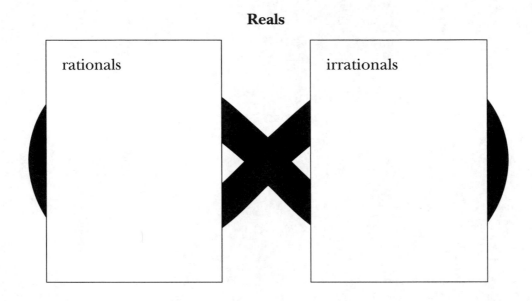

Directions: Which of the two subsets, rationals or irrationals, of the reals do each of the numbers below belong in? Write each number in the appropriate set:

$$0, -2, .3, -4, 8, -2, 5, \pi, \infty, e, 2^{-3}$$

Activity 2.4 Reading Math Symbols

WHAT? Description

Creating a witty short story using math symbols is a good way to reinforce student recognition of these symbols. Students usually think that this activity is fun, and it helps them remember the meaning of the many symbols they will encounter as they learn algebra. Consider these symbols:

Symbol	Meaning	Symbol	Meaning
∞	infinity	$\exists$	there exists
$\approx$	approximately equal to	$\pm$	plus or minus
$\rightarrow$	implies	$\forall$	for all
$\leftrightarrow$	if and only if	$\therefore$	therefore
$\in$	is an element of	$\ldots$	goes on forever in this manner
$\neq$	is not equal to	$\emptyset$	empty set

WHY? Objectives

During this activity, pre-algebra students:

• Reinforce their understanding of the meaning of symbols
• Reflect on and retain math symbols

HOW? Example

In the Land of ∞, $\exists$ a melancholy creature

who was not $\in$ of any particular set or sect.

$\forall$ the creature's desires to be a part of a sect,

she felt she was $\neq$ the other creatures of ∞.

$\leftrightarrow$ she was prettier and smarter, then

she could be an $\in$ of some set besides $\emptyset$.

$\therefore$ she decided that she would $\ldots$ in her humble efforts

$+$ remain a unique creature in the Land of ∞.

Worksheet 2.5 Reading Math Symbols

NAME _____   DATE _____

$2x - 5x + 6x = 3x$ $A(B + C) = AB + AC$ $4 \times 5 = 5 \times 4$ $2(3 + 5)^2 + (-1)^2$ $y = mx + b$

Directions: Use at least six of the symbols below to help you create a story. Write your story in at least four complete sentences. Your story must display the correct meaning of each symbol you use. You may be witty, dramatic, or serious.

Symbol	Meaning	Symbol	Meaning
∞	infinity	$\exists$	there exists
$\approx$	approximately equal to	$\pm$	plus or minus
$\rightarrow$	implies	$\forall$	for all
$\leftrightarrow$	if and only if	$\therefore$	therefore
$\in$	is an element of	$\ldots$	goes on forever
$\neq$	is not equal to	$\emptyset$	empty set

_____

_____

_____

_____

_____

_____

_____

_____

_____

Activity 2.5 Math Glossary

$$2x - 5x + 6x = 3x \quad A(B + C) = AB + AC \quad 4 \times 5 = 5 \times 4 \quad 2(3 + 5)^2 + (-1)^2 \quad y = mx + b$$

WHAT? Description

Asking students to collect the important words or concepts from a chapter or section of text is one of the first steps in building mathematical literacy. Whether by handwriting in their own math notebooks or using computer word processing or spreadsheet programs, students can input the terms from each chapter, so that by the end of this course, they will have created a dictionary or glossary they can use during quizzes or in future courses. It is important to give students a format display of the terms. For example, a student might be asked to give the term's part of speech: noun, verb, adjective, or something else. Then students might be asked to give a definition from the reading or their class notes and a definition or description of their own. A suggested format is given in worksheet 2.6.

WHY? Objectives

In this activity, students create a math glossary giving the term, its part of speech, and a definition. These are the directions to give to them:

- Read an assigned chapter highlighting important concepts.
- List the significant terms, and consider the part of speech of each term.
- Write out the definition from the text.
- Write a personal definition or description of each term.
- Write a phrase or statement using the word correctly.

HOW? Example

These are some sample terms for the glossary:

- Commutative property. *Example:* "You may add 2 + 3 OR 3 + 2, and both will equal 5."
- Associative property
- Distributive property

Worksheet 2.6 Math Glossary

$$2x - 5x + 6x = 3x \quad A(B + C) = AB + AC \quad 4 \times 5 = 5 \times 4 \quad 2(3 + 5)^2 + (-1)^2 \quad y = mx + b$$

Directions: Refer to your lesson on the properties of real numbers to add to your math glossary. Six properties are listed below. Use the example of the commutative property to help you fill in the rest of the matrix. Consider addition to be the operation for each of the properties.

Word or Concept	Part of Speech	Text Definition	My Definition	Example Phrase
Commutative for Addition	*Adjective*	$a + b = b + a$	*You may commute, that is, change the order of the digits being added or multiplied*	*The set of integers is commutative with respect to addition and multiplication.*
Associative				
Distributive				
Identity				
Inverse				
Zero				

Activity 2.6 Semantic Feature Analysis

$2x - 5x + 6x = 3x \quad A(B + C) = AB + AC \quad 4 \times 5 = 5 \times 4 \quad 2(3 + 5)^2 + (-1)^2 \quad y = mx + b$

WHAT? Description

Semantic feature analysis (Baldwin, Ford, & Readance, 1981) is a reading strategy that asks students to complete a matrix showing how various terms and concepts are alike or different. The terms or concepts are related or fall under a particular category. The matrix itself consists of several columns. The first column contains a listing of the terms. The remaining columns contain headings that identify features that the terms or concepts might have in common. See the example in the "How?" section.

WHY? Objectives

During this activity, pre-algebra students:

- Explore features of infinite sets
- Learn the properties of the set of real numbers
- Answer questions about the reals
- Compare and contrast features of certain infinite sets
- Summarize the content on infinite sets from the text and from classroom discussions and lecture
- Refer back to the completed matrix when reviewing for exams

HOW? Example

Each of the following properties requires a set of numbers and an operation. Consider the variables a, b, and c, which refer to any real number unless otherwise stated. The properties are arranged in a semantic feature matrix.

Infinite Sets	Property	Operation(s)	Example or Rule
Reals	Commutative	Addition	$A + B = B + A$
		Multiplication	$AB = BA$
Reals	Associative	Addition	$(A + B) + C = A + (B + C)$
		Multiplication	$(AB)C = A(BC)$
Reals	Distributive	Multiplication over addition or subtraction	$A(B + C) = AB + AC$
Reals	Additive identity	Addition	$A + 0 = A = 0 + A$
Reals	Multiplicative identity	Multiplication	$B \times 1 = 1 \times B$
Reals	Additive inverse	Addition	$A + (-A) = 0 = -A + A$
Reals	Multiplicative inverse reciprocal	Multiplication	$B\left(\frac{1}{B}\right) = 1 = \left(\frac{1}{B}\right)B$ $B \neq 0$

The set of real numbers has a multiplicative inverse (reciprocal) for every number except 0. $A \div 0$ where A is any real number does not exist. Since only one counterexample is required for a property to fail, the multiplicative inverse property does not hold for the set of reals.

☀ Teaching Tip

Once students have been introduced to the properties, it is important that they see them in use. The real number properties are referred to often in later chapters of a pre-algebra text, as well as in later courses. All higher-level mathematics courses are written with the expectation that students have learned this knowledge and are ready to use it in these courses.

Worksheet 2.7 Semantic Feature Analysis: The Infinite Sets of Algebra

NAME _____   DATE _____

$$2x - 5x + 6x = 3x \quad A(B + C) = AB + AC \quad 4 \times 5 = 5 \times 4 \quad 2(3 + 5)^2 + (-1)^2 \quad y = mx + b$$

Directions: Fill in the matrix by writing each of the given infinite sets in each of the three forms. There may or may not be one form that cannot be used for each of the sets.

Infinite Sets	Verbal Description	Roster Form	Set Builder Notation
Real numbers	Set of all numbers that are on the number line.	$\ldots -2, -1, 0, 1, 2 \ldots (-\infty, \infty)$ Interval notation	$\{x \mid x \in Q \text{ or } x \in Q'\}$ This means x is either a rational number Q or x is an irrational number Q' (read Q prime)$\}$
Rational numbers			
Irrational numbers			
Integers			
Whole numbers			
Natural (counting) numbers			

Worksheet 2.8 Semantic Feature Analysis: Features of Infinite Sets

NAME _____ DATE _____

$2x - 5x + 6x = 3x \quad A(B + C) = AB + AC \quad 4 \times 5 = 5 \times 4 \quad 2(3 + 5)^2 + (-1)^2 \quad y = mx + b$

Directions: Fill in the matrix by answering each question yes or no as it pertains to the given large set of numbers. Then answer the questions below the matrix referring to your answers.

Sets	Is an infinite set	Is a subset of the set above it	Has an additive identity in its set	Has a multiplicative identity in its set
Real numbers	Yes	Doesn't apply	Yes	Yes
Rational numbers				
Integers				
Whole numbers				
Natural numbers				
Irrational numbers				

Solutions for Worksheet 2.8

1. Give the additive identity for the set of reals.
2. The set of irrational numbers has an multiplicative inverse for each irrational number. True or false?
3. Give the multiplicative identity for the set of reals.
4. The set of irrational numbers has an additive inverse for each irrational number. True or false?
5. The set of reals can be split into two parts: the rationals and the irrationals. True or false?
6. Give the multiplicative inverse for .3, a rational number.
7. The reals are commutative with respect to division. True or false?

Activity 2.7 In Your Own Words:
A Paraphrasing Activity

$2x - 5x + 6x = 3x$ $A(B + C) = AB + AC$ $4 \times 5 = 5 \times 4$ $2(3 + 5)^2 + (-1)^2$ $y = mx + b$

WHAT? Description

One of the most common excuses that students give for not reading material in their textbooks is that they do not understand the language. This activity helps students target and interpret key concepts. By rewriting portions of mathematical text, students demystify and make personal meaning of mathematical content.

Assign students small portions of the pre-algebra text to read and rewrite in their own words. This activity works equally well with concept definitions, theorems, and examples. Having students read their own versions to each other allows student writers to consider different interpretations and pinpoint misconceptions. If the writing is handed in, you can assess your students' understanding of the material.

WHY? Objectives

During this activity, pre-algebra students:

- Read the content from assigned readings
- Paraphrase the content in their own words
- Share their ideas with peers from the completed paraphrase activity
- Critique each other's translations

HOW? Example

Text	Paraphrase
The real numbers can be partitioned into two infinite sets: the rationals and the irrationals. Moreover, the set of reals has many infinite subsets: rationals, integers, whole numbers, and natural numbers.	The set of real numbers is the largest set, and it has many smaller sets that sit inside of it. But the reals are the most important numbers.

Teaching Tip

Negative exponents give fractions; using the expanded form for a number like 5.26 helps student understand this.

$$5.26 = 5 \times 10^0 \text{ and } 2 \times 10^{-1} + 6 \times 10^{-2} = 5 \times 1 \text{ and } 2 \times \frac{1}{10} + 6 \times \frac{1}{10^{-2}}$$

Worksheet 2.9 In Your Own Words: A Paraphrasing Activity

NAME _____   DATE _____

Directions: Read the passage below. Then write out your understanding of scientific notation. Be clear, and use at least two complete sentences. Be prepared to share your paraphrase with your peers. You may use other sources to help develop your definition.

> José is giving a report on atoms. He found out that an ordinary penny has about 20,000,000,000,000,000,000,000 atoms. And the average size of an atom is about .00000002906 centimeter across.
>
> José finds that both numbers are hard to read and hard to use in calculations. He searches for a way to abbreviate both numbers and finds scientific notation.

Scientific Notation Steps

1. Pick up all the nonzero digits unless the zero(s) are between the nonzero digits.
   Example: $607,000,000 \rightarrow .00009$

2. Write this number as a number x, where $1 \leq x < 10$ by moving the decimal point.
   $6.07 \rightarrow 9.$

3. Finish the process by multiplying by 10 raised to some power—positive for a large number and negative for a small number. The value of the exponent is given by the number of spaces from the original place of the decimal point to the new place that you moved it to make it a number between 1 (inclusive) and 10 (noninclusive).

$$6.07 \times 10^8 \rightarrow 9 \times 10^{-5}$$

4. Write José's numbers in scientific notation:

   $20,000,000,000,000,000,000,000 =$ _____

   $.00000002906 =$ _____

Topics in Integers

WHAT? Introduction

Studying the process of ancient Egyptian multiplication helps pre-algebra students understand the development of the method we use today for multiplying. The first mini-lesson in this chapter introduces this ancient method of multiplying integers. The second mini-lesson discusses integral exponents and the concept of repeated multiplication.

WHY? Objectives

Using the activities in this chapter, pre-algebra students will:

- Determine and collect the important concepts from a lesson for display

- Create concept cards that they can use as study or homework aids

- Use the Frayer method and charts to display the important features, examples, and nonexamples of concepts and processes related to integers or exponents

- Work in small groups to discuss and solve problems and come up with an appropriate rule for solving these types of problems
- Compare and contrast related mathematical concepts or processes and display this knowledge in a premade matrix
- Assess their own knowledge or understanding of integers

Mini-Lesson 3.1   Egyptian Multiplication

CCSS Standards 6.NS: Number Systems

Compute fluently with multi-digit numbers and find common factors and multiples.

The first number systems were developed over four thousand years ago by the Egyptians and Babylonians. This is an ancient Egyptian number:

In our number system this would be 12,425. Each symbol (not necessarily read from left to right) stands for 5 ones, 2 tens, 4 hundreds, 2 thousands, and 1 crooked finger for 10,000. The Egyptians focused on tens because of the number of human fingers and toes, allowing them to use each digit as a tally mark.

The Egyptians understood the usefulness of multiples of numbers as demonstrated in the doubling process used in their multiplication. Let's explore this multiplication system by looking at an example: 18×24.

Consider the first two columns in the table exploring the example. First, we choose 1 and 24 as the multiplicands (a number to be multiplied by another number) and begin doubling each. In the second row, we double 1 to get 2 and double 24 to get 48. Then we double 2 to get 4 and 24 to get 48. This is much like solving equations where if you multiply one side by a number like 2, you must multiply the other side, too.

Continue this doubling until we have some numbers, not necessarily all of them, in the first column that add up to 18. We place a check mark by 2 and 16. Add the two corresponding numbers (across from 2 and 16), 48 and 384, which gives the solution 432. Multiplying, we see $18 \times 24 = 432$.

We could just as well have chosen 1 and 18 to start. Each process gives the same solution. The last two columns in the table show the work using 18 as the multiplier.

Example: $18 \times 24 = 432$

1	24	We check 2 and 16 since $2 + 16 = 18$	1	18
2 √	48 √	48 and 384 correspond to 2 and 16	2	36
4	96	And $48 + 384 = 432$	4	72
8	192	Which is our product	8 √	144 √
16 √	384 √		16 √	288 √
		In the next 2 columns, we use 1 and 18		
18	432	FINAL PRODUCT	24	432

Note the following partial sums: $2 \times 24 = 48$ and $16 \times 24 = 384$. Adding the two partial sums gives $48 + 384 = 432$.

Next, multiply 52×86 using the doubling process:

1	52
2 √	104 doubling 1 and 24
4 √	208 doubling 2 and 104, and so on
8	416
16 √	832
32	1664
64 √	3328
86	4472

Find and add up values from the left column to get 86: $2 + 4 + 16 + 64 = 86$.

Then add the numbers from the right that correspond to arrows checked on the numbers from the left side; for example, 2 corresponds to 104, and 16 corresponds to 832.

Adding $104 + 208 + 832 + 3328 = 4472$ gives the solution.

Checking, $52 \times 86 = 4472$.

The Egyptians knew that they needed a number system to display their inventories of food and animals, measure their land, and record taxes that were paid. However, it was only Egyptian men who learned to read and write numbers and words. Egyptians believed that women's heads were constructed in such a way that they would explode if too much knowledge was put into them!

Teaching Tip

Teaching students to multiply as the Egyptians did is a supplementary mathematical activity. Wait until students have mastered two- or three-digit multiplication and have a good understanding of doubling numbers. Asking students to compare our method with the Egyptian method reveals their understanding of multiplication and leads to some lively classroom discussion.

Activity 3.1 The Writing Is on the Wall

$2x - 5x + 6x = 3x$ $A(B + C) = AB + AC$ $4 \times 5 = 5 \times 4$ $2(3 + 5)^2 + (-1)^2$ $y = mx + b$

WHAT? Description

Elementary teachers often use a word wall or bulletin board to help students learn the spelling and vocabulary of math terms. Your wall will be more useful to students by grouping terms into, for example, the Top Ten, Fabulous Five, or Foremost Four mathematics concepts from each lesson or chapter. Students should be asked to give the key concepts.

Students collect significant pre-algebra or algebra words that they then use to construct their math glossaries and add to their mathematical vocabulary. These concepts are the same words that students will see in all later algebra courses.

WHY? Objectives

During this activity, pre-algebra students:

- Choose key concepts from a section in their textbook or that day's lesson
- Collect words to help construct an algebra glossary over the entire course

HOW? Example

Here are five terms to add to the Fabulous Five Number Forms on the math wall:

Real

Rational

Integer

Whole

Natural

Worksheet 3.1 The Writing Is on the Wall

NAME _____ DATE _____

$2x - 5x + 6x = 3x \quad A(B + C) = AB + AC \quad 4 \times 5 = 5 \times 4 \quad 2(3 + 5)^2 + (-1)^2 \quad y = mx + b$

Directions: Choose ten concepts that involve integers. Look for terms that are related in the same way to the integers. You may use today's lesson or a chapter from your textbook on integers. Then try finding six symbols that may be used with the integers. Write these words under the following categories. Be creative!

Top Ten Terms

Sensational Six Symbols

Activity 3.2 Concept Cards

WHAT? Description

Similar to the concept circle activity described in Chapter One, concept cards are an excellent way for students to create study aids for tests or other assessments. Index cards work well for this activity.

After reading the assigned text and doing any assigned problems, students review the content looking for key concepts. They write the concept on one side of an index card and the definition, features, facts, or theorems regarding the concept on the other side.

Students can use these concept cards to construct a glossary for the entire course or as a study guide for tests or exams. The cards can also become part of a game in which each student reads the definition of a concept and his or her partner guesses the concept described.

WHY? Objectives

During this activity, pre-algebra students:

- Identify the key concepts and terms from the text and use these terms to create concept cards
- Define the concepts in their own words, promoting ownership of the knowledge
- Create a useful study guide for upcoming assessments

HOW? Example

Have students read the chapter on multiplication in their textbooks, paying special attention to the key concepts. When they finish, ask them to construct at least four concept cards as in the example on the next page.

Make sure students remember to write out the definition and important facts or features about the concept on the reverse side of the card.

	Side 1	Side 2
Card 1	Multiplication	Repeated Addition $2 \times 3 = 2 + 2 + 2 = 6$
Card 2	Multiplication symbols	$\times \bullet (\ )$

Activity 3.3 Frayer Model

$2x - 5x + 6x = 3x \quad A(B + C) = AB + AC \quad 4 \times 5 = 5 \times 4 \quad 2(3 + 5)^2 + (-1)^2 \quad y = mx + b$

WHAT? Description

The Frayer model (Frayer, Frederick, & Klausmeier, 1969) is a writing strategy that stresses word categorization, including defining a concept and considering attributes, nonattributes, examples, nonexamples, and other important features. The model presents an excellent reading strategy that requires students to review, reflect on, and study the key concepts of a unit. The four-square model is explained in the example.

WHY? Objectives

During this activity, pre-algebra students:

- Read to search for the facts or features of the concept
- Analyze and write out the attributes and nonattributes of the concept
- Complete a graphic that they can use as a study aid

HOW? Example

Concept = Integers

Your Definition: The set of Integers can be written as $\{\ldots -3, -2, -1, 0, 1, 2, \ldots\}$ Integers are the counting numbers: $1, 2, 3, 4, \ldots$ And the number zero, 0 Along with the opposites of the counting numbers $-1, -2, -3, -4, \ldots$	Important Features: The set of Integers has an Additive identity $= 0$ meaning If A is an integer, then $A + 0 = A = 0 + A$ and Multiplicative identity $= 1$ meaning If B is an integer, then $B \times 1 = B = 1 \times B$
Examples 1 2 −4 1002 −500	Nonexamples $1/2$ $3/3$ .1234 2.5

Worksheet 3.2 Frayer Model

NAME _____   DATE _____

$2x - 5x + 6x = 3x$ $A(B + C) = AB + AC$ $4 \times 5 = 5 \times 4$ $2(3 + 5)^2 + (-1)^2$ $y = mx + b$

Directions: Fill in this sheet by defining "multiplying signed numbers," giving any important rules, and providing examples and nonexamples of this concept. There is not just one right answer for each category.

MULTIPLYING SIGNED NUMBERS

Your definition of:

_____

_____

_____

Rules:

_____

_____

_____

Examples	Nonexamples

Worksheet 3.3 Frayer Model

NAME _____   DATE _____

Directions: Choose a mathematical concept from the chapter on integers. Then fill in the worksheet by defining your concept, giving any important rules, and providing examples and nonexamples of this concept. There is not just one right answer for each category.

Concept = _____

Your definition:

_____

_____

_____

Rules:

_____

_____

_____

_____

Examples	Nonexamples

CCSS Standard 8.EE: Expressions and Equations

Work with radicals and integer exponents.

This lesson explores integers and exponents.

Exponents show repeated multiplication. For example, consider the following exponential expression:

$$2^5 = 2 \times 2 \times 2 \times 2 \times 2 = 32 = \text{the } \textit{value} \text{ of the expression}$$

In the expression, 2^5 is first expressed in expanded form. An exponential expression is also called a *power*. A power has two parts: a base (2 in the example) and an exponent (5 in the example). The expression 2^5 is therefore read as "two to the fifth power." Note that 2 is written out five times, then multiplied to arrive at the value of 32.

 Teaching Tip

- Any number to the first power is the number itself:
  $2^1 = 2, x^1 = x$
- Any number raised to the 0 power is 1:
  $3^0 = 1, y^0 = 1$

This table shows the different forms of certain exponential expressions, including how the exponential expression should be read.

Exponential Form	Expanded Form	Verbal Form or Verbal Expression	Numerical Form
5^0	1	Five raised to the zero power	1
15^1	15	Fifteen to the first power	15
4^2	$4 \cdot 4$	Four to the second power or Four squared	16
$(.2)^3$	$(.2)(.2)(.2)$	Two-tenths to the third power or Two-tenths cubed	$(.2)(.2)(.2) = .008$

-7^4	$-(7 \times 7 \times \times 7 \times 7)$	The opposite of the quantity seven to the fourth power	$-2{,}401$
$(-3)^5$	$(-3)(-3)(-3)(-3)(-3)$	Negative three to the fifth power	-243
-2^2	$-(2)(2)$	The opposite of 2 squared	-4

Some students may confuse the expression $-n^2$ with $(-n)^2$. The n in $-n^2$ represents the base, and therefore n is the value squared, while the negative or opposite sign remains. In $(-n)^2$, the value $(-n)$ is the base and is squared, making the solution a positive number. This will be true for all exponents that are integers. For example,

$$-3^4 = -(3)(3)(3)(3) = -81$$
$$(-3)^4 = (-3)(-3)(-3)(-3) = 81$$

Remember that exponents are used when simplifying certain arithmetic and algebraic expressions. To evaluate these expressions requires following a certain order, referred to as the *order of operations*:

1. Do the inside parentheses first.
2. Do the exponents from left to right.
3. Do the multiplication and division from left to right.
4. Do the addition and subtraction from left to right.

A popular and easy way to remember the order with which to do the operations is to remember the acronym PEMDAS:

P PLEASE (parentheses)
E EXCUSE (exponents)
M MY (multiplication)
D DEAR (division)
A AUNT (addition)
S SALLY (subtraction)

The operations are completed from left to right. Multiplication and division are done left to right as either comes up; for example, $2 \times 8 \div 2 \times 2 = 16 \div 2 \times 2 = 8 \times 2 = 16$. The same applies to addition and subtraction.

Many expressions can be simplified and equations solved by using the order of operations and combining like terms when using variables as in the following examples:

1. $2(3+5)^2 + (-1)^3 = 2(8) + (-1) = 16 + (-1) = 15$
2. $-4^2 - 3^3 + 2^6 = -16 - 27 + 64 = 21$
3. $2x^2 + 14x^3 - x^2 - 4x^3 = x^2 + 13x^3$. Note here that x^2 and x^3 are not like terms and cannot be combined.

· · ·

$20x - 2(4 - 2x) = 7 + 3x - +6$ (simplify using PEMDAS on both sides of the equal sign first)

$20x - 8 + 4x = 13 + 3x$

$24x - 8 = 13 + 3x$ (combine like terms)

$21x = 21$ (subtract 3x from both sides)

$x = 1$ (divide both sides by 21)

Activity 3.4 What's My Rule?

WHAT? Description

For this guided discovery activity, students, working alone or in groups, are presented with several examples of a certain mathematical concept or rule. Then they brainstorm and write the rule or conjecture (that is, what they think the rule might be). Next, they solve problems using their conjecture.

This activity is best completed with a teacher or teacher's aide available to check for the accuracy of rules.

WHY? Objectives

During this activity, pre-algebra students:

- Discover mathematical rules while observing and completing several problems that use the rule
- Practice writing and using certain mathematical conjectures
- Work cooperatively to arrive at a well-expressed and accurate rule

HOW? Examples

The rule here is "Raising to a power means repeated multiplication of the exponential notation":

1. $2^3 = 2 \times 2 \times 2 = 8$
2. $(-1)^4 = (-1)(-1)(-1)(-1) = 1$
3. $(1/2)^2 = 1/2 \times 1/2 = 1/4$
4. $(.3)^5 = .3 \times .3 \times .3 \times .3 \times .3 = .00015$
5. $5^5 = 5 \times 5 \times 5 \times 5 \times 5 = 3125$

Worksheet 3.4 What's Your Rule?
Scientific Notation

NAME _____ DATE _____

Directions: After studying the examples, try solving the unfinished problems. Then write a rule in a complete and clearly constructed sentence that explains how you solve scientific notation problems.

$3{,}200 = 3.2 \times 10^3$	$.0034 = 3.4 \times 10^{-3}$
$4{,}560{,}000 = 4.56 \times 10^6$	$.0506 = 5.06 \times 10^{-2}$
$2{,}031{,}000{,}000 = 2.031 \times 10^9$	$.0002003 = 2.003 \times 10^{-4}$
$239{,}000 = 2.39 \times 10^5$	$.04008 = 4.008 \times 10^{-2}$
$81 = 8.1 \times 10$	$.999 = 9.99 \times 10^{-1}$
$900012 = 9.00012 \times 10^5$	$.009120 = 9.12 \times 10^{-3}$
$4{,}100{,}000 = $ _____	$.00051 = $ _____
$995 = $ _____	$.995 = $ _____
3 million $ = $ _____	two-tenths $ = $ _____
$256 = $ _____	$.000256 = $ _____
What's my rule?	What's my rule?
_____	_____
_____	_____
_____	_____
_____	_____
_____	_____

Worksheet 3.5 What's Your Rule? Exponent Laws

NAME _____   DATE _____

$$2x - 5x + 6x = 3x \quad A(B + C) = AB + AC \quad 4 \times 5 = 5 \times 4 \quad 2(3 + 5)^2 + (-1)^2 \quad y = mx + b$$

Directions: After studying the examples, try solving the unfinished problems. Then write a rule in a complete and clearly constructed sentence that explains how you simplify each type of exponential problems.

$2^2 \cdot 2^4 = 2^6$	$(X^2)^3 = X^5$
$X^3 \cdot X^2 = X^5$	$(X^3)^0 = X^0 = 1$
$a^3 \cdot a^4 \cdot a^2 = a^9$	$(a^5)^2 = a^{10}$
$3^0 \cdot 3^1 = 3^1$	$(2x^3)^2 = 4x^6$
$x^2\, y^3\, x^3\, y^4 = x^5\, y^7$	$(-3m^4)^3 = -27m^{24}$
$a^2\, a^3 a^1 =$ _____	$(a^3\, b^4)^5 =$ _____
$x^2\, x^3 =$ _____	$(x^4)^2 =$ _____
$2^3 \cdot 2^2 \cdot 2^1 =$ _____	$(-2^2\, b^3)^2 =$ _____
What's my rule?	What's my rule?
_____	_____
_____	_____
_____	_____
_____	_____
_____	_____
_____	_____

Activity 3.5 Comparison-and-Contrast Matrix

$2x - 5x + 6x = 3x$ $A(B + C) = AB + AC$ $4 \times 5 = 5 \times 4$ $2(3 + 5)^2 + (-1)^2$ $y = mx + b$

WHAT? Description

Students can use the comparison-and-contrast matrix (Vacca & Vacca, 1999) to compare and contrast related features of related concepts. Choose the concept and features, and ask students to fill in the blank squares. They can then use the completed matrix as a study guide or turn it in as an assignment. Students' answers may be objective or subjective depending on the concepts or features to be compared.

WHY? Objectives

During this activity, pre-algebra students:

- Research and reflect on the similarities and differences of related mathematical concepts
- Receive feedback from their teacher about the validity of the facts in their matrices

HOW? Example

This matrix shows the different forms for an exponential expression—how they differ and how they are alike. The tables can be used in different ways to compare and contrast the features of an algebraic concept.

Forms Base	Exponential Expression	Expanded Form	Numerical Value
2	2^0	1	1
2	2^1	2	2
2	2^2	2×2	4
2	2^3	$2 \times 2 \times 2$	8
2	2^4	$2 \times 2 \times 2 \times 2$	16

Worksheet 3.6 Comparison-and-Contrast Matrix: Integral Exponent

NAME _____ DATE _____

$$2x - 5x + 6x = 3x \quad A(B + C) = AB + AC \quad 4 \times 5 = 5 \times 4 \quad 2(3 + 5)^2 + (-1)^2 \quad y = mx + b$$

Directions: Fill in the matrix (the first row has been filled in as an example). You and your peers might find different answers.

	Negative Exponents	Zero Exponent	Positive Exponents
History; who and when invented	Arabs c. 800 A.D.	Arabs c. 1000 A.D.	Greeks c. 250 B.C.
Uses in math today			
Numerical example			
Example			

Worksheet 3.7 Comparison-and-Contrast Matrix: Exponent Laws

NAME _____ DATE _____

Directions: Fill in the matrix (the first row has been filled in as an example). You and your peers might find different answers.

	Rule	**Example**	**Common Error**
Product rule	$B^5 = B^2 \, B^3$ $(B \cdot B)(B \cdot B \cdot B)$ *When multiplying exponential expressions, add the exponents*	$x^2 x^4 = x^{2+4} = x^6$	*Multiplying exponents instead of adding*
Quotient rule			
Power rule			

Worksheet 3.8 Comparison-and-Contrast Matrix: Multiplication

NAME _____   DATE _____

$2x - 5x + 6x = 3x$ $A(B + C) = AB + AC$ $4 \times 5 = 5 \times 4$ $2(3 + 5)^2 + (-1)^2$ $y = mx + b$

Directions: Fill in the matrix. You and your peers might find different answers.

	Egyptian Multiplication (ancient method)	Hindu-Arabic Multiplication (current method)
When was it invented?		
What are its basic rules?		
Show how it works.		
Find 12×26.		
What are its limitations and problems?		
What are its values and merits?		

Activity 3.6 Knowledge Ratings

WHAT? Description

Knowledge ratings allow students to assess their prior understanding of a topic (Blachowicz, 1986). Using this activity, your students will be able to see the value in measuring their own progress and determining where they need to study more. The survey headings for knowledge rating charts may take various forms depending on the topic of the chart, as the example in this section shows.

WHY? Objectives

During this activity, pre-algebra students:

- Fill out knowledge ratings charts
- Target problem areas and make study plans
- Point out personal problem areas to teachers

HOW? Example

Rate how much you know about integer operations (positive and negative) by placing an X in the cell under the heading that best describes how you would rate your understanding of the subjects in the first column.

Positive and Negative Integers	A lot!	Some!	Nothing!
Adding			
Subtracting			
Multiplying			
Dividing			

Worksheet 3.9 Knowledge Rating Activity for Exponent Rules

NAME _____   DATE _____

$2x - 5x + 6x = 3x \quad A(B + C) = AB + AC \quad 4 \times 5 = 5 \times 4 \quad 2(3 + 5)^2 + (-1)^2 \quad y = mx + b$

Directions: How much do you know about these terms? Place an X in the spaces for which you agree.

Exponent Rules	I know a lot about this topic!	I remember some of the rules.	I know nothing at all about this topic.
Product rule			
Quotient rule			
Negative exponents			

Number Theory

WHAT? Introduction

The Common Core State Standards recommend that sixth-grade students be able to write and interpret numerical expressions and find common factors and multiples. This chapter introduces these concepts, using reading and writing strategies and activities to reinforce understanding and may even allow students to appreciate the playfulness and aesthetics of numbers. Students and teachers often consider number theory to be the fun part of math! The stronger the base that students have with operations involving prime and composite numbers and factors, the easier it will be to apply this knowledge to algebra.

WHY? Objectives

In this chapter, pre-algebra students will:

- Develop and solve number riddles
- Learn to paraphrase content
- Construct magic squares
- Work with semantic feature analysis tables to display their knowledge of number theory concepts

Mini-Lesson 4.1   Divisibility Rules

CCSS Standard 6.NS: Number System

Compute fluently with multi-digit numbers and find common factors and multiples.

Divisibility rules offer shortcuts for determining if a number is divisible by another number rather than having to do long division. Knowledge of these rules gives pre-algebra students a useful tool for mental math and problem solving.

A *prime* number is a positive whole number that has only 1 and itself as factors (divisors). For example, the number 2 has only 1 and 2 as its factors, and 13 has only 1 and itself as its factors. Thus, 2 and 13 are prime numbers. A *composite* number has more than two factors. For example, the number 4 has 1, 2, and 4 as its factors, making 4 a composite number. The number 1 is a special case: it is considered to be neither prime nor composite, because $1 = 1 \times 1 \times 1 \times 1 \ldots$ Note that 1 is the only factor of itself.

Divisibility is a useful property of whole numbers. For example, 2 divides 8 and 5 divides 15.

 Teaching Tip

It's important not to confuse the divisibility symbol (|) with the fraction bar, as "/" in the fraction $\frac{25}{102}$ or 25/102. In fact, we would say here that 25 does not divide 102, since 25 and 102 have no factors in common. Be careful to sketch the "divides" sign as a vertical line to reinforce the difference.

Consider the following:

- 2|14 is true, since $2 \times 7 = 14$.

- 7|20 is false since there is no whole number that when multiplied by 7 gives 20. The numbers 7 and 20 are said to be "relatively prime," meaning they have no factors in common except 1.

- 1|0 is true since $1 \times 0 = 0$. Care must be taken when dealing with 0 and divisibility, because in general a number cannot be divided by 0.

- 0|6 is false since there is no whole number that when multiplied by 0 gives 6.

The *divisibility rule* is that, in general, a whole number a divides another whole number b, a|b, iff there exists a whole number n so that $a \times n = b$.

Iff means "if and only if." It implies you could rewrite the rule with the condition reversed. For example, $2|8$ implies $2 \times 4 = 8$, and $2 \times 4 = 8$ implies $2|8$. Therefore, we write $2|8$ iff $2 \times 4 = 8$.

Knowing many of the following divisibility rules is useful when mentally dividing large numbers by small numbers. For example, 52,266 is divisible by 2 since the unit's last digit is even. It is also divisible by 6. Let's see if we can determine why.

Divisibility by 2: A number is divisible by 2 iff its last digit is 0, 2, 4, 6, or 8.

Divisibility by 3: A number is divisible by 3 iff the sum of the digits is divisible by 3, since $5 + 4 + 0 + 0 + 6 = 15$ and $3|15$. Also, 15 is divisible by 3 since $1 + 5 = 6$.

Divisibility by 4: A number is divisible by 4 iff the number formed by the last two digits is divisible by 4. *Example:* 13,564 is divisible by 4 because $4|64$. Note that 52,266 is not divisible by 4 since 4 does not divide 66.

Divisibility by 5: A number is divisible by 5 iff the last number is 5 or 0. Note that 52,266 is not divisible by 5, but a number like 6050 is divisible since the unit's last digit is 0.

Divisibility by 6: A number is divisible by 6 iff it is divisible by 2 and divisible by 3. Remember that "and" means it must happen in both. Recall the number 52,266 from above. We can now see 52,266 is divisible by 6 since $2|52,266$ and $3|52,266$.

Divisibility by 8: A number is divisible by 8 iff the last three digits form a number divisible by 8. Note that 52,266 is not divisible by 8 since 266 is not divisible by 8. Also, 4 does not divide 52,266 so 8 could not divide it.

Divisibility by 9: A number is divisible by 9 iff the sum of the digits is divisible by 9. Note that 52,266 is not divisible by 9 since $5 + 2 + 2 + 6 + 6 = 21$ and 9 does not divide 21. Note also that 3 may divide a number, but that does not mean 9 will.

Divisibility by 10: A number is divisible by 10 iff its unit's digit is a 0. In fact, a number is divisible by 10^n iff the last n digits of the number are 0s. Note that 4800 is divisible by $10^2 = 100$ since it ends with two 0s and 250,000 is divisible by $10^4 = 10,000$ since it ends with four 0s.

The number 142,460 is divisible by 2, 3, 4, 5, 6, and 10 but *not* 9:

- It is divisible by 2 since the unit's digit is 0.
- It is divisible by 3 since the sum of the digits, $1 + 4 + 2 + 4 + 6 + 0 = 15$, and 3 divides 15.
- It is divisible by 4 since the last two digits give the number 60, and 4 divides 60.
- It is divisible by 5 since 142,460 ends with zero.
- It is divisible by 6 since 2 and 3 are relatively prime, and both divide 142,460.
- It is *not* divisible by 9 since the sum of its digits is not divisible by 9.
- It is divisible by 10 since the unit's digit is a 0.

When you need to find and use the quotient, divisibility rules help only up to a point. But if you are interested in finding the factors of a multidigit number, then knowing all of the basic divisibility rules makes the process go much faster.

Activity 4.1 Number Riddles

WHAT? Description

This activity may be used with many different mathematical processes but works especially well with the divisibility rules. Students work in pairs to create riddles based on the model described below.

WHY? Objectives

During this activity, pre-algebra students:

- Work in pairs to create number riddles
- Review and discuss the divisibility rules
- Compete and cooperate to find more complex riddles to solve
- Use or learn to use numbers in a creative manner

HOW? Example

Here is a sample number riddle: "I am thinking of a number whose digits add up to a number divisible by 9. What other numbers must divide my number?" *Answer:* 1 and 3.

Pairs of students can share and solve each other's riddles, discussing how they found the answers.

Worksheet 4.1 Number Riddles Using the Divisibility Rules

$2x - 5x + 6x = 3x$ $A(B + C) = AB + AC$ $4 \times 5 = 5 \times 4$ $2(3 + 5)^2 + (-1)^2$ $y = mx + b$

Directions: Try to answer the following number riddles.

1. I am thinking of a number that is divisible by 6. What other whole numbers will divide my number?

2. My number is also divisible by 4 and less than 20. Can you guess my number?

3. I am thinking of a number that is divisible by 12. What other whole numbers will divide my number?

4. My number is also divisible by 11, but NOT divisible by 8. Can you find my number?

5. Is there more than one possibility for riddle 4? _____ If so, what is that possibility?

6. I am thinking of a number that is divisible by 9 and between the numbers 30 and 50. Must the number be divisible by 3? _____ By 2? _____

7. If the number in riddle 6 is NOT divisible by 4, what is my number?

Now it's your turn. With a partner, brainstorm and write your riddle. Trade riddles with another pair, and try to solve each other's. When you are finished, discuss the problem and create another one.

_____

_____

_____

_____

Solutions for Worksheet 4.1

NAME _____   DATE _____

$$2x - 5x + 6x = 3x \quad A(B + C) = AB + AC \quad 4 \times 5 = 5 \times 4 \quad 2(3 + 5)^2 + (-1)^2 \quad y = mx + b$$

1. I am thinking of a number that is divisible by 6. What other whole numbers will divide my number? **2 and 3**

2. My number is also divisible by 4 and less than 20. Can you guess my number? **12**

3. I am thinking of a number that is divisible by 12. What other whole numbers will divide my number? **1, 2, 3, 4, 6**

4. My number is also divisible by 11, but NOT divisible by 8. Can you find my number? **132**

5. Is there more than one possibility for riddle 4? **Yes**. If so, what is that possibility? **924**

6. I am thinking of a number that is divisible by 9 and between the numbers 30 and 50. Must the number be divisible by 3? **Yes**. By 2? **Not necessarily**

7. If the number in riddle 6 is NOT divisible by 4, what is my number? **45**

Activity 4.2 In Your Own Words: A Paraphrasing Activity

$$2x - 5x + 6x = 3x \quad A(B + C) = AB + AC \quad 4 \times 5 = 5 \times 4 \quad 2(3 + 5)^2 + (-1)^2 \quad y = mx + b$$

WHAT? Description

One of the most common excuses that students give for not reading material in their textbook is that they do not understand the language. This activity helps students target and interpret key concepts. By rewriting mathematical passages, students demystify and make personal meaning of mathematical content.

Assign students small portions of the pre-algebra text to read and rewrite in their own words. This activity works equally well with concept definitions, theorems, and examples. Having students read their own versions to each other allows student writers to consider different interpretations and pinpoint misconceptions. If writing is handed in, you can assess your students' understanding of the material.

Rewording or rewriting the divisibility rules is a good way to remember them.

WHY? Objectives

During this activity, pre-algebra students:

- Paraphrase the content on assigned portions of the text
- Focus on the important ideas in the content or lesson
- Share their paraphrasing activity with peers

HOW? Example

Text

There are three types of positive integers: prime numbers, composite numbers, and "1." Prime numbers only have two factor, 1 and itself. Composite numbers have more than two factors. The number 1 is unique since it does not fit in either the primes or the composites.

Paraphrase

Prime numbers are like 2: it has only 1 and 2 as its factors; 13, for example, has only 1 and 13 as its factors. Composite numbers are not prime like the number 4, which has three factors: 1, 2, and 4. The number 1 is different: it has only one factor, and that is 1!

Worksheet 4.2 In Your Own Words: A Paraphrasing Activity

NAME _____ DATE _____

$2x - 5x + 6x = 3x$ $A(B + C) = AB + AC$ $4 \times 5 = 5 \times 4$ $2(3 + 5)^2 + (-1)^2$ $y = mx + b$

Directions: In your pre-algebra book, reread the lesson on divisibility rules. Then follow the prompts below, paraphrasing (putting into your own words) the content.

Rewrite the divisibility rule for 2 in your own words.

_____

_____

_____

_____

How are the divisibility rules for 3 and 9 alike and different?

_____

_____

_____

If a number is divisible by 6, with what other numbers is it necessarily divisible?

_____

_____

The rules for divisibility for 4 and 8 are very similar. Explain.

_____

_____

_____

Can you make a rule for divisibility by 12 or by 24? What makes these rules similar to the rule for 6?

_____

_____

_____

Activity 4.3 Magic Square

WHAT? Description

The magic square activity combines a matching activity with the intrigue and mathematics of a magic square (Vacca & Vacca, 1999). The format of the matching activity consists of two columns, one for concepts and one for definitions, facts, examples, or descriptions. As the student solves the matching activity, he or she places the numbers in the proper square inside the magic square.

A	B	C
D	E	F
G	H	I

To check their answers, students add the numbers in each row, in each column, and on each diagonal. These sums should be equal. This sum is referred to as the square's "magic number." Sometimes only the numbers in the rows will sum up to the magic number and one or more diagonal contains values that do not add up to the magic number.

Any mathematics topic that has a list of related features or rules, such as the divisibility rules, lends itself nicely to a matching exercise. In turn, a magic square gives a superb format for finding and posting the correct matches from the matching exercise.

WHY? Objectives

During this activity, pre-algebra students:

- Reinforce the meanings of concepts or words
- Learn about the features of a magic square

HOW? Example

The magic squares below are 3-by-3 unit squares. Notice that the cells in this particular magic square contain all whole numbers from 1 to 9 with no repeats. When you add the numbers in each column, in each row, and in each diagonal, your sum is 15. This number is called the *magic number*.

8	1	6
3	5	7
4	9	2

Worksheet 4.3 Magic Square: Divisibility Rules

NAME _____   DATE _____

$2x - 5x + 6x = 3x$ $A(B + C) = AB + AC$ $4 \times 5 = 5 \times 4$ $2(3 + 5)^2 + (-1)^2$ $y = mx + b$

Directions: Select the best answer for each of the concepts on the left from the numbered rules on the right. Put the number in its proper place in the magic square. Add each row and add each column. If these sums are the same number, you have found the magic number and correctly matched concepts with their rules.

Concepts	Rules
A. Divisibility by 2	1. Sum of even-numbered digits minus sum of odd-numbered digits is divisible by 11.
B. Divisibility by 8	2. Unit's digit is 0 or 5.
C. Divisibility by 3	3. The number formed by the last three digits is divisible by 8.
D. Divisibility by 11	4. Sum of digits is divisible by 3.
E. Divisibility by 6	5. Number is divisible by 2 and 3.
F. Divisibility by 10	6. Number formed by the last two digits is divisible by 4.
G. Divisibility by 4	7. Sum of all digits is divisible by 9.
H. Divisibility by 9	8. Unit's digit is 0, 2, 4, 6, or 8.
I. Divisibility by 5	9. Unit's digit is 0.

A	B	C
D	E	F
G	H	I

Magic number =

Copyright © 2013 by John Wiley & Sons, Inc.

Pre-Algebra Out Loud

Mini-Lesson 4.2 Greatest Common Denominator and Least Common Multiple

CCSS Standard 6.NS: Number System

Compute fluently with multi-digit numbers and find common factors and multiples.

The greatest common factor and the least common multiple have many applications in mathematics. First, we discuss the greatest common divisor (or factor).

A *common factor* is a multiplier or divisor shared by two or more numbers. The *greatest common factor* (often called the greatest common divisor, GCD) is the largest factor that two or more numbers or terms have in common. The GCD is used to simplify fractions. *Example:* $\frac{12}{56} = 4 \times \frac{3}{4} \times 14 = \frac{3}{14}$.

There are two methods for finding the GCD of two or more numbers: the all-factors method and the prime factorization method.

All-Factors Method for Finding the GCD

1. Write out (or list) all the whole number factors for each of the numbers.
2. Circle or underline all common factors.
3. Select the greatest of the common factors.

Example: Find the GCD for the numbers 60, 96, and 156, using the all-factors method:

$$60: \underline{1, 2, 3, 4}, 5, \underline{6}, 10, \underline{12}, 15, 20, 30, 60$$
$$96: \underline{1, 2, 3, 4, 6}, 8, \underline{12}, 16, 24, 32, 48, 96$$
$$156: \underline{1, 2, 3, 4, 6, 12}, 13, 26, 39, 52, 78, 156$$

Therefore, the GCD of 60, 96, and 156 = 12.

☀ Teaching Tip

Some students want to stop writing down factors when they find one factor that the numbers have in common; for example, 4 is a common factor of 60, 96, and 156. However, to find the *greatest* common factor, they must list all factors of each number.

Prime Factorization Method for Finding the GCD

1. Find all the prime factors for each of the numbers. Write each number as a product of its prime factors.
2. Express all factors that repeat in exponential form.
3. Find all the common prime factors to their least power.

Check by multiplying the factors they have in common to arrive at the GCD.

 Teaching Tip

Every positive integer can be expressed as a unique product of prime numbers.

Example: $24 = 2 \times 12 = 2 \times 2 \times 6 = 2 \times 2 \times 2 \times 3$. This product of primes is equal *only* to 24.

Example: Find the GCD for 60, 96, and 156, using the prime factorization method. The last row gives the prime factorization for each of the numbers in the first row.

60	96	156
2×30	2×48	2×78
$2 \times 2 \times 15$	$2 \times 2 \times 24$	$2 \times 2 \times 39$
$2 \times 2 \times 3 \times 5$	$2 \times 2 \times 2 \times 12$	$2 \times 2 \times 3 \times 13$
	$2 \times 2 \times 2 \times 2 \times 6$	
	$2 \times 2 \times 2 \times 2 \times 2 \times 3$	
$2^2 \times 3 \times 5$	$2^5 \times 3$	$2^2 \times 3 \times 13$

The numbers 60, 96, and 156 have 2^2 and 3 in common. Therefore, the GCD is $2^2 \times 3 = 12$.

Next, we consider the *least common multiple* (LCM), also called the *least common denominator* (LCD), when adding or subtracting fractions.

A *common multiple* is a composite number that two or more numbers (not counting 1) divide. The *least common multiple* is the smallest number that two or more numbers can divide into.

When adding fractions, we need to find a common denominator and change the fractions into 1s with the common denominator in order to add the numerators.

As with the GCD, there are two methods for finding the LCM: the all-multiples method and the prime factorization method.

All-Multiples Method for Finding the LCM

1. Find several (at least five to start) of the multiples for two or more numbers.
2. Select the least of the multiples that the numbers have in common and you will discover the LCM.

Example: Find the LCM for 8, 12, and 30 using the all-multiples method:

8: 8, 16, 24, 32, 40, 48, 56, 64, 72, 80, 88, 96, 104, 112, <u>120</u>
12: 12, 24, 36, 48, 60, 72, 84, 96,108, <u>120</u>
30: 30, 60, 90, <u>120</u>, 150, 180, 210

By the all-multiples method, the LCM is equal to 120. It is usually written LCM (8, 12, 30) = 120.

 Teaching Tip

It is impossible to list all multiples of any number. So have students list all multiples up to the one multiple that the first two numbers have in common. Then they should list multiples of the third number until they find one that is in common with all three numbers. Stress that they may have to repeat this process more than once to find the LCM.

Prime Factorization Method for Finding the LCM

1. Find all the prime factors for each of the numbers. Write each number as a product of its prime factors.
2. Express all factors that repeat in exponential form.
3. Find all the different factors to their greatest powers.
4. Multiply, and you will have the LCM.

Example: Find the LCM using the prime factorization method. Recall the prime factorization for the numbers 60, 96, and 156:

60	96	156
2×30	2×48	2×78
$2 \times 2 \times 15$	$2 \times 2 \times 24$	$2 \times 2 \times 39$
$2 \times 2 \times 3 \times 5$	$2 \times 2 \times 2 \times 12$	$2 \times 2 \times 3 \times 13$
	$2 \times 2 \times 2 \times 2 \times 6$	
	$2 \times 2 \times 2 \times 2 \times 2 \times 3$	
$2^2 \times 3 \times 5$	$2^5 \times 3$	$2^2 \times 3 \times 13$

The different factors are 2, 3, 5, and 13. The different factors to their greatest powers are 2^5, 3, 5, and 13. The LCM is the product of all the different factors (to their greatest power), which is $2^5 \times 3 \times 5 \times 13 = 6240$.

Example: Find the LCM (12, 30, 42) using the prime factorization method:

12	30	42
2×6	2×15	2×21
$2 \times 2 \times 3$	$2 \times 3 \times 5$	$2 \times 3 \times 7$
$2^2 \times 3$	$2 \times 3 \times 5$	$2 \times 3 \times 7$

Therefore, the LCM $(12, 30, 42) = 2^2 \times 3 \times 5 \times 7 = 420$.

Activity 4.4 Semantic Feature Analysis

WHAT? Description

Semantic feature analysis (Baldwin, Ford, & Readance, 1981) is a reading strategy that asks students to complete a matrix showing how various terms and concepts are alike or different. The terms or concepts are related or fall under a particular category. The matrix itself consists of several columns. The first column contains a listing of the terms. The remaining columns contain headings spelling out or asking about features that the terms or concepts might have in common.

The GCF and LCM have comparable features, and the method for finding either one is similar. To use the prime factorization method to find either the GCF or LCM, first factor each of the numbers into a product of primes. In the all-factors and all-multiples methods, list all factors for the GCF and as many multiples needed to find the LCM. Using the semantic feature analysis is a good forum for displaying the similarities and the differences of these processes.

WHY? Objectives

During this activity, pre-algebra students:

- Compare and contrast features of related mathematical concepts
- Summarize this information
- Refer back to the completed matrix when reviewing for exams

HOW? Example

The following table displays an analysis of certain divisibility rules. Write yes or no (the answers are given in this example) in the cell according to the features along the top with the types of numbers along the left-most column.

Divisibility Rule	Uses Sums of Its Digits	Uses Parts of the Number	Uses a Combination of Other Divisibility Rules
Divisible by 2	No	Yes	No
Divisible by 3	Yes	No	No
Divisible by 4	No	Yes	No
Divisible by 5	No	Yes	No
Divisible by 6	Yes	Yes	Yes
Divisible by 8	No	Yes	No
Divisible by 9	Yes	No	No
Divisible by 10	No	Yes	No

Worksheet 4.4 Semantic Feature Analysis

NAME _____   DATE _____

$2x - 5x + 6x = 3x \quad A(B + C) = AB + AC \quad 4 \times 5 = 5 \times 4 \quad 2(3 + 5)^2 + (-1)^2 \quad y = mx + b$

Directions: Answer yes or no to the question asked in each cell. In the right-hand column, write out another name for each process.

	May Use Prime Factorization to Find	May Be Used to Add or Subtract Fractions	May Be Used to Factor	Write Another Name for the Process
Least common multiple (LCM)				
Greatest common divisor (GCD)				

Number Theory

Worksheet 4.5 Semantic Feature Analysis

NAME _____   DATE _____

The number 5 can be expressed in one rectangle model, meaning a rectangle divided into five connected and equal-sized units or squares. If the rectangle is a horizontal strip, its row by column sizes are written as 5 by 1. If the rectangle is a vertical strip, then it is expressed as 1 (row) by 5 (columns, or 1 by 5). Since the only factors for 5 are 5 and 1, it has only one rectangle model:

1	2	3	4	5

This rectangle model for 5 is 1 row by 5 columns. We will consider 5 columns by 1 row to have the same rectangular array.

The following two arrays, 2×2 and 1×4, represent the number 4:

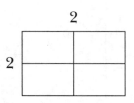

Directions: Fill in the table on the next page with the factors and the number of rectangles (factors) that can be formed by the indicated number. Then use your results to answer the questions following the table.

Note that each rectangular model represents a pair of factors.

The dimensions column gives each number's pair of factors, which are also the dimensions of each rectangular array. For example, 2 has only two factors: 1 and 2. Thus, 2 has one rectangular array with the dimensions 1 by 2—one row and two columns.

Worksheet 4.5 continued

Number	Dimensions	Number of Rectangle = Factors
2	1×2	1
3	1×3	1
4	$1 \times 4, 2 \times 2$	2
5		1
6		
7		
8		
9		
10		
11		
12	$1 \times 12, 2 \times 6, 3 \times 4$	3
13		
14		
15		
16		
17		
18		
19		
20		

Questions:

• Which types of numbers—primes, composites, squares, and soon—have only one rectangle model?

_____

• Which types of numbers have more than one rectangle model?

_____

Extend the table to the number 36 and see if you can draw some other conclusions about the different types of numbers and their rectangular models or factors.

Fractions, Decimals, and Percents

WHAT? Description

Many students have difficulty learning and understanding how to work with fractions. Research shows that students who have a poor comprehension of what a fraction is will struggle with such operations as addition and subtraction problems that include fractions or fractional coefficients. The goal of this chapter is to help students understand that a fraction is a part of a whole or a part of a set. In addition, the lessons in this chapter explore the relationship of fractions, decimals, and percentages.

WHY? Objectives

Using the activities in this chapter, pre-algebra students:

- Repeat exercises that illustrate a rule and discover that rule
- Respond to writing prompts that target certain features about fractions, decimals, and percentages
- Compare and contrast various features about fractions
- Build semantic word maps that demonstrate and display fractional forms and concepts

CCSS Standard 6.RP: Ratios and Proportional Relationships

Understand ratio concepts and use ratio reasoning to solve problems.

A fraction has two parts: a numerator and a denominator. The denominator gives the size of the fraction as in a circle (represented as a pizza) divided into one-fourths (see below). The numerator gives the number of parts. Another way to think of this is in terms of the top number and bottom number:

- The top number (numerator) counts.
- The bottom number (denominator) gives what is being counted.
- We can see that 3 *of the* $\frac{1}{4}$*s gives* $\frac{3}{4}$.
- 4 *of the* $\frac{1}{4}$*s gives* $\frac{4}{4} = 1$.

We always write fractions in their simplest form.

Just about everyone has some experience dividing pizza or a pie into pieces. Let's assume each circle's pieces are all the same size. Consider the pizzas (circles) below divided into fourths, halves, and eighths.

$\frac{1}{4}$ is $\frac{1}{4}$ of the whole pizza! Two $\frac{1}{4}$s is one-half of the pie.

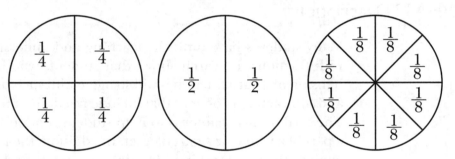

☀ Teaching Tip

Sketching these circles and the fraction bars on the board or using manipulatives or cut-outs will reinforce students' understanding of fractions as parts of a whole. Be sure to write the fractions inside the circles.

It is clear to see many relationships (equivalences) between the pieces of the circles such as these:

$$\frac{1}{2} = two \ \frac{1}{4}s$$

$$\frac{1}{2} = four \ \frac{1}{8}s$$

$$Three \ \frac{1}{4}s = six \ \frac{1}{8}s$$

$$Three \ \frac{1}{4} \ s = six \ \frac{1}{8}s$$

How many equivalent fractions can be found between the parts of the pizzas at the left?

To gain a deeper comprehension of these concepts, students can observe equivalencies by sketching fraction bars. Compare the following bars to see the same fractions given above:

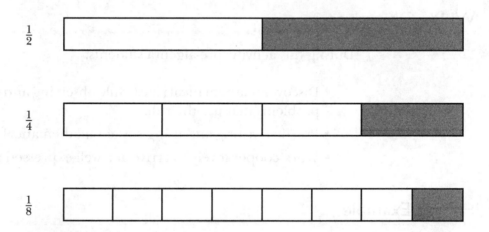

Another way to think about fractions is to consider the ratio of two amounts of objects—for example, $\triangle \triangle \triangle$ compared to $\triangle \triangle \triangle \triangle \triangle = 3$ to $5 \equiv \frac{3}{5}$.

If we think of these five stars as a whole set, then we can consider two of the stars to be $\frac{2}{5}$ of the set.

We explore in this chapter several other ways to express fractions.

Activity 5.1 What's My Rule?

$2x - 5x + 6x = 3x$ $A(B + C) = AB + AC$ $4 \times 5 = 5 \times 4$ $2(3 + 5)^2 + (-1)^2$ $y = mx + b$

WHAT? Description

This is a guided discovery activity. Working alone or in groups, students are presented with several examples of a certain mathematical concept or rule. Then they brainstorm and write up the rule or conjecture, that is, what they think the rule might be. Students then solve problems using their conjecture. This activity is best completed with a teacher or teacher's aide available to check for accuracy.

There are many facts and rules regarding fractions and their forms. Worksheets 5.1, 5.2, 5.3, and 5.4. illustrate some of these features.

WHY? Objectives

During this activity, pre-algebra students:

- Discover mathematical rules while observing and completing several problems that use the rule
- Practice writing and using certain mathematical conjectures
- Work cooperatively to arrive at a well-expressed and accurate rule

HOW? Example

The goal here is to determine the rule from this set of equalities:

1. $.25 = 25\%$
2. $.005 = .5\%$
3. $1.25 = 125\%$
4. $15 = 1500\%$
5. $.000102 = .0102\%$

My rule: To convert decimal fractions into percentages, move the decimal point two places to make the number look larger. Then add a % sign on the right of the number.

Worksheet 5.1 To Terminate or Not

NAME _____ DATE _____

Directions: Consider the examples below, and fill in the rest of the rows. Then give your rule.

Simplified Fraction	Denominator	Prime Factorization of Denominator	Decimal Equivalent	Does It Terminate?
$\dfrac{1}{10}$	10	$2 \cdot 5$	.1	yes
$\dfrac{3}{40}$	40	$2 \cdot 2 \cdot 2 \cdot 5$	.075	yes
$\dfrac{1}{3}$				
$\dfrac{1}{24}$				
$\dfrac{11}{125}$				
$\dfrac{13}{200}$				
$\dfrac{2}{15}$				

My rule: _____

_____

_____

_____

Activity 5.2 Writing Prompts

WHAT? Description

Math teachers regularly use writing prompts as a form of authentic assessment or to gauge their students' understanding of a concept. Writing prompts, such as those that follow, allow students to think about their own learning and how well they understand specific mathematical concepts. Writing prompts may be used in students' math journals or as a beginning or an ending to a lesson.

Consider the following prompts:

- Today I learned that . . .
- Something we did in math class today reminded me of . . .
- I am still not sure about . . .
- Outside class, I can use what we learned today when . . .
- I am confident when I do . . .
- I get confused when I . . .
- It would help me in class if . . .

Other prompts may be more focused on the content of the lesson:

- Explain what *simplest form* means.
- Compare a decimal to a fraction. How are they alike, and how are they different?
- Explain the role of the numerator and the denominator in a fraction.

WHY? Objectives

During this activity, pre-algebra students:

- Think about their own learning and practice metacognition, the study and understanding of how we learn and process information
- Practice writing and communicating about mathematics
- Compare and contrast certain mathematical or algebraic concepts

HOW? Example

Writing prompts may be as simple as "Fractions are . . . " or as complex as "The reason I struggle with adding and subtracting fractions is . . . "

Worksheet 5.2 Writing Prompts for a Lesson in Fractions

NAME _____ DATE _____

$$2x - 5x + 6x = 3x \quad A(B + C) = AB + AC \quad 4 \times 5 = 5 \times 4 \quad 2(3 + 5)^2 + (-1)^2 \quad y = mx + b$$

What I like about learning fractions is:

_____

_____

_____

Something about fractions that I need to practice more is:

_____

_____

_____

_____

Fractions should be written in simplified form because:

_____

_____

_____

The difference between the numerator and the denominator is:

_____

_____

_____

_____

CCSS Standard 6.NS: Number System

Apply and extend previous understandings of numbers to the system of rational numbers.

Writing Fractions as Decimals

To find the decimal equivalent of a certain fraction, we divide. *Example:* 3 divided by 4 is $\frac{3}{4}$, which gives .75. We can read $\frac{15}{20}$ as 15 divided by $20 = .75$.

Simplified fractions "terminate," or have a finite number of terms, only if their denominator is a 2 or 5 or both. *Example:* The fraction $\frac{1}{40}$ has a denominator of 40, which has a prime factorization of $2 \times 2 \times 2 \times 5$. The decimal for the fraction is .025.

A fraction such as $\frac{1}{3}$ will not terminate but will have a repeating pattern. Another example is $\frac{5}{24}$. The denominator has a prime factorization: $2 \cdot 2 \cdot 2 \cdot 3$. Also, the decimal fraction is .2083333 ... and does not terminate.

All simplified fractions have a decimal that either terminates or a pattern that repeats forever.

 Teaching Tip

Fractions are always written in their simplified form, often called lowest terms. A fraction is in lowest terms when both numerator and denominator have no factors in common. Another way to say this is the top and bottom of a fraction are "relatively prime."

Writing Decimals as Fractions

Reading a decimal correctly provides an excellent way to write a fraction.

Decimal	Verbal	Fraction
.51	fifty-one hundredths	$\frac{51}{100}$
1.253	one and two hundred fifty-three thousandths	$1\frac{253}{1000}$

A decimal greater than 1 can be written as a mixed number or as an improper fraction, that is, a fraction whose numerator is greater than its denominator.

A special case is a decimal that has a repeated pattern, for example, .25252525 ...

To find its equivalent simplified fraction, set n = .25252525...

$100n = 25.252525$ multiply both sides by 100 (because decimals are part of 100)

$\underline{-n = .2525252}$ subtract from the equation above

$99n = 25$ the .25252525 ... is subtracted off

$n = \frac{25}{99}$ giving us a fraction

Remind students that they may need to simplify fractions, because solutions must always be in lowest terms:

$$.5 = \frac{5}{10} = \frac{1}{2}$$
$$.225 = \frac{9}{40}$$

Writing Decimals as Percents

To write decimals as percents, move the decimal point two places to make the decimal look larger and add the percent sign: $.25 = 25\%$ and $.05 = 5\%$, for example. Another way to explain the rule is this: "To change a decimal to a percent, move the decimal point to the right." Having to memorize which direction the decimal moves, left or right, may cause confusion. It's best to remember the percent always looks larger than the decimal and the decimal always looks smaller than the percent. In fact, they are equivalent to each other, as is their fractional representation. This means we multiply by 100. *Percent* means "per one hundred" so 25% is 25 parts out of 100.

Examples

Convert .056 to a percent: $.056 = 5.6\%$

Convert 125% to a decimal: $125\% = 1.25$

Convert .05 to a percent and then to a simplified fraction:
$.05 = 5\% = 5$ per $100 = \frac{5}{100} = \frac{1}{20}$

☀ Teaching Tip

Always write fractions in simplified form. If you do this from the beginning of discussing fractions, students will realize it is part of the process and will always do it this way.

Activity 5.3 Comparison-and-Contrast Matrix

WHAT? Description

Students can use the comparison-and-contrast matrix (Vacca & Vacca, 1999) to compare and contrast related features of related concepts. Choose the concept and features, and ask students to fill in the blank squares. The completed matrix may then be used as a study guide or turned in as an assignment. Students' answers may be objective or subjective depending on the concepts or features to be compared.

WHY? Objectives

During this activity, pre-algebra students:

- Research and reflect on the similarities and differences of fractions, decimals, and percents
- Complete a comparison-and-contrast matrix and use the matrix as a study guide
- Receive feedback about any misconceptions they have of the meaning of the concepts in their matrices

HOW? Example

Worksheets 5.3 and 5.4 will give students practice in this activities.

Worksheet 5.3 Comparison-and-Contrast Matrix: Rational Numbers

NAME _____   DATE _____

$$2x - 5x + 6x = 3x \quad A(B + C) = AB + AC \quad 4 \times 5 = 5 \times 4 \quad 2(3 + 5)^2 + (-1)^2 \quad y = mx + b$$

Directions: Fill in the cells in the following matrix. Each row will have four forms for each fractional number. The different forms are given in the first row, at the top of each column.

Verbal Form	Simplified Fractional Form	Decimal Form	Percent Form
Twenty-five eighths			
	$\dfrac{3}{40}$		
		5.25	
			.025

Worksheet 5.4 Comparison-and-Contrast Matrix: Fractions

NAME _____   DATE _____

$$2x - 5x + 6x = 3x \quad A(B + C) = AB + AC \quad 4 \times 5 = 5 \times 4 \quad 2(3 + 5)^2 + (-1)^2 \quad y = mx + b$$

Directions: Draw a sketch of the given fraction, and write a complete sentence using the description of the fraction.

Fraction	Sketch of a Part of a Circle	Sentence Using Fraction as a Part of	Sketch of a Ratio of Objects	Sentence Using Fraction as a Ratio of
$\dfrac{1}{4}$				
$\dfrac{3}{5}$				
$\dfrac{5}{6}$				

Activity 5.4 Semantic Word Maps

$2x - 5x + 6x = 3x$ $A(B + C) = AB + AC$ $4 \times 5 = 5 \times 4$ $2(3 + 5)^2 + (-1)^2$ $y = mx + b$

WHAT? Description

Semantic word maps are used to depict and display the relationships between key concepts and terms. These word maps often resemble flowcharts or webs connecting mathematical terms. Arrows connect related concepts and often display a hierarchy of the term, where one term is a set and the others are subsets of that set. For example, if algebra is the main set, then equations, variables, and constants are all parts of the set or subsets of the set "algebra." After students have completed their semantic word maps, pose critical-thinking questions—questions that go beyond the calculations and use higher-order thinking skills regarding the relationships of the concepts.

WHY? Objectives

During this activity, pre-algebra students:

- Explore relationships between mathematical concepts and terms
- See the hierarchy of key concepts
- Create study guides displaying key concepts

HOW? Example

Consider the following related concepts:

fractions	improper fractions
mixed numbers	decimal fractions
numerator	denominator

Text boxes and arrows can be used to display the connections or hierarchy of terms:

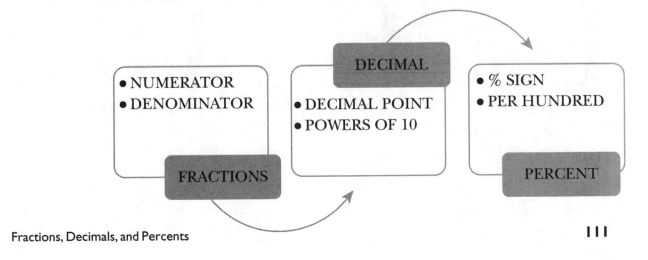

Worksheet 5.5 Semantic Word Map

NAME   DATE

$$2x - 5x + 6x = 3x \quad A(B + C) = AB + AC \quad 4 \times 5 = 5 \times 4 \quad 2(3 + 5)^2 + (-1)^2 \quad y = mx + b$$

Directions: Use the following terms in the given word map to show the relationship of the terms. You do not need to use all of the terms.

- fraction, decimal, percent
- rational numbers, real numbers
- numerator, denominator
- division, quotient
- ratio, proportion

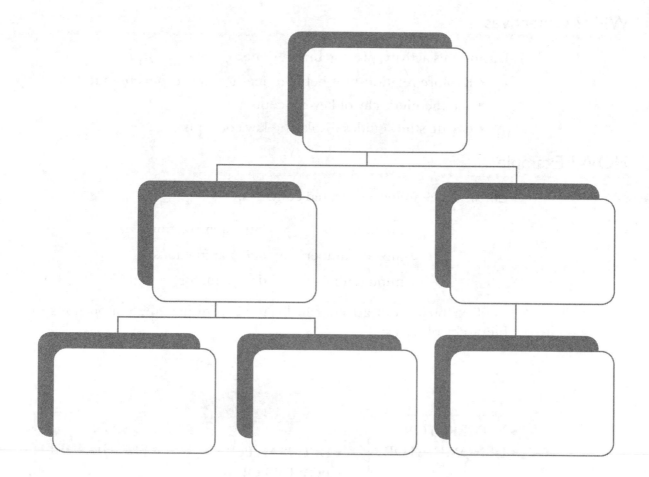

Pre-Algebra Out Loud

Worksheet 5.6 Semantic Word Map

NAME _____   DATE _____

Directions: Place fraction words in the circle. Choose at least six terms that are related to fractions. Use your textbook to find and choose the words that will help you create a semantic word map inside the circle.

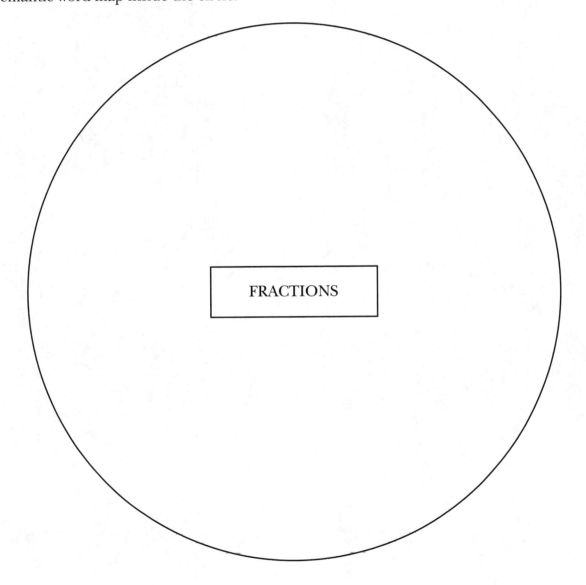

$$2x - 5x + 6x = 3x \quad y = mx + b$$

Equations and Inequalities

WHAT? Introduction

In 2000, the National Council of Teachers of Mathematics recommended that the mathematics curriculum include explorations of algebraic concepts and processes so that students can develop confidence in solving linear equations and investigating inequalities. Today one of the ten goals of the sixth-grade Common Core State Standards requires students to reason about and solve one-variable equations and inequalities. Pre-algebra students learn the basics of algebra early in the course and practice higher-order arithmetic skills so they can learn to solve multistep equations and related applications.

This chapter contains two mini-lessons: the first on solving multistep, one-variable equations and the second on solving one-variable inequalities. The reading and writing strategies in this chapter involve multistep equations, inequalities, and applications using linear equations.

WHY? Objectives

Using the activities in this chapter, pre-algebra students:

- Learn to paraphrase math content
- Examine, write out, and explain each step in the process of an algebraic algorithm or method of operation

- Translate algebra into words
- Create a written word problem that involves a linear equation in one variable
- Collect words and concepts to build a math glossary
- Write a biography on a notable mathematician

Mini-Lesson 6.1 Solving Multistep Equations

CCSS Standard 7.EE: Expressions and Equations

Solve real-life and mathematical problems using numerical and algebraic expressions and equations.

An equation is a mathematical sentence in which the left side is equal to the right side. Think of an equation as a balance scale, where the quantities on the left and right sides of the equal sign balance or are equal in value. Moreover, if we perform an operation on one side, we must perform the same operation on the other side so that the equation stays in balance.

Example 1

$2x - 4 = 10$	The goal is to undo everything done to x using the opposite operation
$2x - 4 = 10$	Add 4 to each side (opposite of adding 4)
$+4 + 4$	Simplify
$\dfrac{2x}{2} = \dfrac{14}{2}$	Divide both sides by 2 (opposite of multiplying by 2)
$x = 7$	Solution

Example 2

$8x - 9 = 2x + 15$	Our goal is to undo everything done to x
$\underline{2x \qquad - 2x}$	Subtract equal amounts $-2x$
$6x - 9 = 15$	Simplify
$\underline{+9 \quad +9}$	Add equal amounts 9
$\underline{6x = 24}$	Simplify
$\quad 6 \qquad 6$	Divide by same divisor 6
$x = 4$	Solution

The great thing about solving equations is that we can check our solutions. If placing 4 into the original equation gives a true statement, then it is the correct solution.

Check

$$8(4) - 9 = 2(4) + 15, \text{ which gives}$$
$$32 - 9 = 8 + 15, \text{ which gives}$$
$$23 = 23 \checkmark, \text{ which gives a true statement.}$$

Linear equations generally have one solution. Linear equations in one variable are equations with a single variable, like x. The variable may have coefficients and the equation may contain constants.

Some equations have no solutions, and some have an infinite number—for example:

$2(x + 2) = 2x - 6$	Simplify by distributing the 2
$2x + 4 = 2x - 6$	
$-2x \qquad -2x$	Subtract 2x from both sides
$4 = -6$	Clearly a false statement

Therefore, there is no value for x that will make this equation $2(x + 2) = 2x - 6$ true, and there is no solution.

Here's another example:

$3x - 9 = 3(x - 3)$	Distribute the 3
$3x - 9 = 3x - 9$	This is an identity
$-3x \qquad -3x$	Subtract 3x from both sides
$-9 = -9$	A true statement

This equation is an identity because the left side is identical to the right side when simplified. Although both sides of the original identity do not look the same, any number substituted for the variable will make the equation true and eventually give an identical equation, like $-9 = -9$ above. The solution set for an identity is infinite and consists of all the real numbers.

When solving any algebraic equation, use a series of equivalent equations—equations that have the same solutions, often referred to as solution sets.

☀ Teaching Tip

After students learn to solve equations, they may make this mistake: when asked to simplify the expression $24x - 14x - 10$, they add an equal sign and 0 to it. Then they solve it. Algebraic expressions get simplified and equations get solved.

Simplified: $24x - 14x - 10 = 10x - 10$

Activity 6.1 In Your Own Words:
A Paraphrasing Activity

$$2x - 5x + 6x = 3x \quad A(B + C) = AB + AC \quad 4 \times 5 = 5 \times 4 \quad 2(3 + 5)^2 + (-1)^2 \quad y = mx + b$$

WHAT? Description

One of the most common excuses that students give for not reading material in their textbooks is that they do not understand the language. This activity helps students target and interpret key concepts. By rewriting portions of mathematical text, students demystify and make personal meaning of mathematical content.

Assign students small portions of the pre-algebra text to read and rewrite in their own words. This activity works equally well with concept definitions, theorems, and examples. Having students read their own versions to each other allows student writers to consider different interpretations and pinpoint misconceptions. If the writing is handed in, you can assess your students' understanding of the material.

WHY? Objectives

During this activity, pre-algebra students:

- Read the content from assigned readings
- Paraphrase the content in their own words
- Share their ideas with peers from the completed paraphrase activity
- Discuss and critique each other's translations

HOW? Examples

Example 1

Textbook: The solution set for an equation that is unsolvable is the empty set.

Student paraphrase: Some equations have no solutions so their solution set is empty and it looks like { }.

Example 2

Textbook: Linear equations always have x raised to the first power. These equations have one, none, or an infinite number of solutions and are said to be consistent, inconsistent, or dependent (respectively).

Student paraphrase: Linear equations never have x squared or cubed; x is always by itself. A consistent equation has one solution. An inconsistent equation has no solutions. And the dependent equation has an infinite number of solutions.

Worksheet 6.1 In Your Own Words:
A Paraphrasing Activity

NAME _____   DATE _____

$2x - 5x + 6x = 3x$ $A(B + C) = AB + AC$ $4 \times 5 = 5 \times 4$ $2(3 + 5)^2 + (-1)^2$ $y = mx + b$

Directions: Review mini-lesson 6.1 on solving multistep equations. Then use the prompts below to help you paraphrase the material. Be clear, and use complete sentences. Be prepared to share your translation with your peers. You may use other sources to help develop your answers.

My definition of an algebraic equation is:

_____

_____

_____

My understanding of solving multistep equations is:

_____

_____

_____

Show how to solve the following equation: $5x + 2 = 16 - 2x$:

_____

_____

_____

Activity 6.2 Method of Operation

$2x - 5x + 6x = 3x \quad A(B + C) = AB + AC \quad 4 \times 5 = 5 \times 4 \quad 2(3 + 5)^2 + (-1)^2 \quad y = mx + b$

WHAT? Description

Most mathematical content consists of processes. Students need to know the "how-tos," or methods for arriving at or simplifying solutions. Asking students to write out methods of operation (MO) reinforces their understanding of how to solve problems and helps them consider the fine points of exceptions to the rule.

You might ask students to write out the MO for finding the solutions for a linear inequality. We want students to understand the algorithm for solving inequalities, as well as why the algorithm works. Students should be encouraged to write out the MO as if they were talking to another student who is just learning this process. This motivates clear and concise work and helps each student consider useful algebraic vocabulary.

WHY? Objectives

During this activity, pre-algebra students:

- Complete an MO for an algebraic process
- Use a completed MO to conduct an algebraic process
- Share their MOs with their peers (optional)

HOW? Example

Ask students to write out the MO for finding the solution for a multistep linear equation in one variable: $ax + b = c$.

1. Add or subtract any constants from both sides of the equation.
2. If there are terms on both sides of the equation that contain the variable, add or subtract to get only one term containing the variable.
3. If the variable has a coefficient, divide both sides of the equation by that number.
4. You should have the variable equal a number that is the solution.

Worksheet 6.2 Method of Operation

NAME _____   DATE _____

$2x - 5x + 6x = 3x$ $A(B + C) = AB + AC$ $4 \times 5 = 5 \times 4$ $2(3 + 5)^2 + (-1)^2$ $y = mx + b$

1. Write out the method of operation for the following inequality:
   $Ax + B > C$, where A is a positive number

   _____

   _____

   _____

   _____

   _____

2. Give the method of operation for finding the solution of any inequalities of the forms
   $x > k$ or $x \geq k$ in interval notation.

   _____

   _____

   _____

   _____

3. Sandy is at least 21 years old. Her brother Sam is 2 years younger than she is. Using x
   as the variable that represents Sam's age, write and solve the inequality that represents
   Sam's age. Then write the method of operation for solving this inequality and give the
   solution in interval notation.

   _____

   _____

   _____

   _____

Mini-Lesson 6.2 Solving Linear Inequalities

CCSS Standard 6.EE: Expressions and Equations

Reason about and solve one-variable equations and inequalities.

Solving a linear inequality is very similar to solving a linear equation; the difference is that the solution for an inequality includes a range of numbers. To get started, consider the definition of a linear inequality in one variable. A linear inequality in one variable can be expressed in the form: $ax + b < 0$, where a and b are real numbers but $a \neq 0$.

The inequality sign will be one of the following: $<, >, \leq,$ or $\geq$.

Symbol	Meaning
$<$	less than
$>$	is greater than
$\leq$	is less than or equal to
$\geq$	is greater than or equal to

A number line can be used to visualize solutions to inequalities in one variable—for example, ≤ -2:

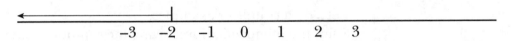

The inequality can also be expressed in what is called *interval notation,* a form of writing a solution that contains an interval of infinite numbers that are solutions to the inequality. Parentheses or brackets are used to enclose the solutions between two numbers or a number and positive or negative infinity. The symbol for positive infinity is $+\infty$ and for negative infinity $(-\infty)$. Infinity in mathematics is an abstract symbol for "goes on forever." *Positive infinity* means the solutions or numbers get large, in fact, very large. *Negative infinity* is an abstraction for a very, very small number, a negative number.

The parentheses in interval notation tell us that the numbers given inside are not part of the solution, and brackets [], as shown in the examples below, show the numbers are included in the solution set. A parenthesis is always placed next to the positive or negative infinity symbol $-\infty-$:

$x \leq -2$ is expressed as $(-\infty, -2]$; -2 is included in the solution

$x < -2$ is expressed as $(-\infty, -2)$; -2 is not part of the solution

$x \geq -2$ is expressed as $[-2, +\infty)$; -2 is included in the solution

$x > -2$ is expressed as $(-2, +\infty)$; -2 is not part of the solution

The same opposite operations used for solving equations are used to solve inequalities. However, there is one more rule: when multiplying or dividing by a negative number during opposite operations, change the direction of the inequality sign—for example:

$$-2x > 6$$

Dividing by -2 gives $x < -3$.

In interval notation, this is $(-\infty, -3)$.

Checking a value, -4, in this range gives $-2(-4) = 8$, which is clearly greater than 6, as the original inequality states.

☀ Teaching Tip

Students often ask why the direction of the inequality sign switches for multiplication and division of negative coefficients (multipliers).

You can explain it in this way: "Consider $3 < 4$. Now multiply each side by the positive number 2, which gives $6 < 8$, a true statement. However, multiplying by -2 gives $-6 < -8$, which is not true unless we switch the signs."

Let's do a couple of examples.

Solve the inequalities for x giving the solution as an inequality and in interval notation.

Example 1

$$3x - 6 \leq 9$$
$$\underline{+6 + 6}$$
$$\frac{3x}{3} \leq \frac{15}{3}$$
$$x \leq 5 \quad (-\infty, 5]$$

Example 2

$$7 - 2x > -7$$
$$\underline{-7 \qquad -7}$$
$$\frac{-2x}{-2} > \frac{-14}{-2}$$

$x < 7$ (remember to change the direction of the inequality sign)

$(-\infty, 7)$

A compound inequality is an inequality that has two inequality signs, usually less than ($<$) signs (for example, $-2 < x < 4$), and is expressed in interval notation as $(-2, 4)$. $-2 < x < 4$ is read "x is greater than negative 2 but less than positive 4," or " x is a number between negative 2 and 4."

Here is an example for solving a compound inequality:

$$-3 < x + 2 < 9$$
$$-3 - 2 < x + 2 - 2 < 9 - 2 \text{ (subtract 2 from all three sides)}$$
$$-5 < x < 7 \text{ or, in interval notation, } (-5, 7)$$

Activity 6.3 Translating Words into Algebra

$2x - 5x + 6x = 3x$ $A(B + C) = AB + AC$ $4 \times 5 = 5 \times 4$ $2(3 + 5)^2 + (-1)^2$ $y = mx + b$

WHAT? Description

This lesson asks students to translate English phrases or sentences into algebraic expressions or equations. This activity is best used as a precursor to activity 2.4, in which students create their own word problems. To be successful at this activity, pre-algebra students must work with their knowledge of basic ideas and concepts of algebra or use their textbooks or concept circles to find definitions and descriptions of math and algebra concepts.

WHY? Objectives

During this activity, pre-algebra students:

- Practice translating algebraic symbols into words
- Learn more about how linear applications are constructed and solved
- Practice deciphering mathematical word problems
- Practice using and translating algebra concepts into real-world problem solving
- Write out the definitions of the terms *expression*, *equation*, and *inequality* and identify the differences among them

HOW? Examples

Here are three examples of translations:

- Five times a number plus six $\rightarrow$ $5x + 6$ is an *expression*.
- One-half of 10 times a number and 3 is twice that number $\rightarrow$ $\frac{1}{2}(10x + 3) = 2x$ is an *equation*.
- A number is at most 13 times $\frac{2}{3}$. The number $\rightarrow$ $x \leq 13 \left(\frac{2}{3} x\right)$ is an *inequality*.

Worksheet 6.3 Translating Words Into Algebra

NAME _____ DATE _____

$2x - 5x + 6x = 3x \quad A(B + C) = AB + AC \quad 4 \times 5 = 5 \times 4 \quad 2(3 + 5)^2 + (-1)^2 \quad y = mx + b$

Directions: Translate each of the following phrases or sentences into algebraic terms. Label each problem as an expression, equation, or inequality by circling the correct term. There is no need to solve any of the equations or inequalities. Use as many numbers and symbols as possible in your translation. If you feel there is more than one way to translate your phrase, choose one way and write it out in numbers and symbols.

1. The product of 13 and a number, all divided by 2 = _____

    Circle one: Expression   Equation   Inequality

2. The sum of five times a number and 2 = _____

    Circle one: Expression   Equation   Inequality

3. The opposite of a negative 3 minus 2 times a number = _____

    Circle one: Expression   Equation   Inequality

4. Seven times the quantity of 2 and a number is at least 4 = _____

    Circle one: Expression   Equation   Inequality

5. A number is at most the quotient of 40 and negative 4 = _____

    Circle one: Expression   Equation   Inequality

6. Write an example like the ones above of your own and translate it into algebra. Label it an expression, equation, or inequality.

    _____

    _____

    _____

    _____

Activity 6.4 Writing Word Problems

WHAT? Description

Often students find solving word problems difficult and confusing. This activity asks students to create their own applications, which allows them to look at solving written problems from a different angle. Students do best with this activity when they can look at examples of a "good" problem and a "bad" one. It should be clear how many variables are needed and whether the problem should be linear or quadratic, for example.

Students work in pairs or small groups of three or four to create the problem. Problems can be written on the board, on overhead transparencies, or typed on a word processor that can be projected onto a screen. Each group may then exchange problems and work out solutions on the board. While doing this activity, students learn:

- They must work backward to get the numbers to work out.
- They must choose the words they use carefully so others can understand the question.
- They must understand *why* the problem works and not just *how*.

WHY? Objectives

During this activity, pre-algebra students:

- Work together and research word problems
- Create a word problem that can be solved
- Exchange problems with their classmates and try to solve them
- See how problems are constructed

HOW? Example

The following is a student-created problem and a good example of what types of words should or should not be used for your assignment:

A swimming pool in the shape of a rectangle is 35 feet by 15 feet. A deck around the pool is the same width all around. The swimming pool and the deck form a large rectangle with an area of 800 square feet. Find the width of the deck

Worksheet 6.4 Creating a Word Problem

NAME _____ DATE _____

$2x - 5x + 6x = 3x \quad A(B + C) = AB + AC \quad 4 \times 5 = 5 \times 4 \quad 2(3 + 5)^2 + (-1)^2 \quad y = mx + b$

Directions: One way to create a word problem is to start with an equation and construct a situation or story using the equation. It will be simpler to write a story or word problem about events or things that are important or interesting to you.

For example, think of a situation for which $5 + x = 23$ might be appropriate. First, decide what you want the variable x to stand for; for example, x = number of dollars earned. Then you notice that this equation has only one operation in it, addition. Now you can add something from your own experience—for example:

> x represents Ashley's weekly allowance that she gets for vacuuming the house. She recently got a raise of $5 and now receives a weekly allowance of $23. Find her original allowance.

Use the following equations to create word problems. You will share these with your peers.

$X - 4 = 10$

_____

_____

_____

$3x = 24$

_____

_____

_____

$2x + 1 = 9$

_____

_____

_____

Worksheet 6.5 Creating a Word Problem

NAME _____   DATE _____

One way to create a word problem is to ask a question that requires a numerical solution. Then fill in the facts needed to answer that question. Here is an example:

Question: What are the width and length of a rectangle with a perimeter of 146 feet?

Word problem: A rectangular-shaped room has a length of 16 feet and a perimeter of 146 feet. Find the width of the room.

Solution: Using the perimeter formula for a rectangle, $P = 2l + 2w$, gives:

$146 = 2(16) + 2w$

$114 = 2w$

$w = 57$ feet

Assignment: Create word problems for the following questions.

1. How tall is the tallest boy in our class?

   _____

   _____

   _____

   _____

   _____

2. How many magic tricks can Adrian perform in 2 hours?

   _____

   _____

   _____

   _____

   _____

Activity 6.5 Math Glossary

$$2x - 5x + 6x = 3x \quad A(B + C) = AB + AC \quad 4 \times 5 = 5 \times 4 \quad 2(3 + 5)^2 + (-1)^2 \quad y = mx + b$$

WHAT? Description

Asking students to collect important words or concepts from a chapter or section of text is one of the first steps in building mathematical literacy. Whether by handwriting in their own math notebooks or using computer word processing or spreadsheet programs, students can input the terms from each chapter. By the end of this course, they will have created a pre-algebra dictionary or glossary that they can use during quizzes or in future courses.

It is important to give students a format for the display of the term. For example, a student might be asked to give the term's part of speech (noun, verb, adjective, or something else). Then the student might be asked to give a definition from the reading or class notes and a definition or description of his or her own.

WHY? Objectives

During this activity, pre-algebra students:

- Create a math glossary giving the term, its part of speech, and definition
- Read an assigned chapter highlighting important concepts
- List the significant terms, and consider each term's part of speech
- Write out the word's definition
- Brainstorm, create, and write a personal definition or description of each term
- Write a phrase or statement using the word correctly

HOW? Example

This example gives one term regarding equations and inequalities:

Term: solution

Part of speech: noun

Text definition: answer to a problem or question

My definition: the number you get when solving an equation

Sentence: The solution to the equation $2x = 6$ is 3.

Worksheet 6.6 Math Glossary

NAME _____   DATE _____

$$2x - 5x + 6x = 3x \quad A(B + C) = AB + AC \quad 4 \times 5 = 5 \times 4 \quad 2(3 + 5)^2 + (-1)^2 \quad y = mx + b$$

Directions: Refer to our lesson on algebraic equations to create part of a math glossary. Choose at least five concepts or words and fill in the matrix. One is done for you.

Word or Concept	Part of Speech	Text Definition	My Definition	Example Phrase
Equation	Noun	A mathematical sentence stating that two quantities are equal.	A math sentence with variables and numbers separated by an equal sign that you have to solve.	A linear equation usually has one solution.

Activity 6.6 Biographies of Algebraists

$2x - 5x + 6x = 3x \quad A(B + C) = AB + AC \quad 4 \times 5 = 5 \times 4 \quad 2(3 + 5)^2 + (-1)^2 \quad y = mx + b$

WHAT? Description

A good way to understand algebra is to explore how the field of algebra came to be. Several mathematicians contributed to the development of the field of mathematics that came to be algebra.

Researching a mathematician's life and contributions helps students appreciate the step-by-step development of the various algebraic theorems and processes. Several of the mathematicians and their contributions to the field of algebra are listed below. Assign students a particular mathematician or have them choose one of their liking. Ask students to share their biographies with the class to broaden the learning experience.

Mathematician	Contribution
Pythagoras	Number theory
Euclid	Euclidean geometry and axioms
Erastosthenes	Good approximation of the circumference of the Earth at the equator
Archimedes	Considered greatest mathematical genius of antiquity
Gauss	Algebraic patterns and formulas
Fibonacci	Sequences and medieval algebra
Descartes	Cartesian coordinate system

WHY? Objectives

During this activity, pre-algebra students:

- Research a mathematician of their choosing and take notes
- Construct a write-up of a mathematician's life story
- Explore and prepare a brief presentation on their mathematician's math inventions

The assignment of a biography of a mathematician should include a format for the write-up. For example, each biography might consist of the following parts:

- Early life
- Education and career
- Family or social life
- Algebraic contributions
- Later life

The rubric on the next page may be used to grade student work.

Grading Rubric

$$2x - 5x + 6x = 3x \quad A(B + C) = AB + AC \quad 4 \times 5 = 5 \times 4 \quad 2(3 + 5)^2 + (-1)^2 \quad y = mx + b$$

Content score (10 possible) = _____

Contains accurate information on mathematician?   1   2   3   4   5

Correctly explains the mathematics introduced?   1   2   3   4   5

COMMENTS:

_____

_____

_____

Mechanics score (10 possible) = _____

Grammar, spelling, clarity, transitions, introduction, conclusion?

1   2   3   4   5

Contains required parts and follows guidelines? 1   2   3   4   5

COMMENTS:

_____

_____

_____

Resources score (5 possible) = _____

Format? Amount of sources, library source?   1   2   3   4   5

COMMENTS:

_____

_____

_____

Final grade = _____

Worksheet 6.7 Math Biographies

NAME _____   DATE _____

Directions: Choose one of the following mathematicians and write a biography to share in class.

Mathematician	Contribution
Pythagoras	Number theory, figurative numbers
Euclid	Axioms, geometry
Erastosthenes	Good approximation of circumference of Earth at equator
Archimedes	Considered greatest mathematical genius of antiquity; volume of the sphere; physics; "Eureka!"
Gauss	Algebraic patterns and formulas, law of large numbers
Fibonacci	Fibonacci Sequence, medieval algebra, The Rabbit
Descartes	Cartesian coordinate system

Guidelines

1. Each biography must contain the following parts:
   - Early life
   - Education and career
   - Family or social life
   - Mathematical contributions
   - Later life
   - Resource list

2. Use at least three different sources, with at least one from the school's library.

3. Your biography should be a minimum of four typed double-spaced pages and a maximum of six typed double-spaced pages in length.

4. The last page should be a bibliography in a consistent format.

5. Identify in the biography your mathematician's influence on the field of algebra.

Pre-Algebra Out Loud

Visualizing Algebra by Graphing Lines

WHAT? Introduction

A good way to help your students visualize algebra is to introduce the basics of graphing linear equations and allow them to create graphs and build equations from these graphs. The Common Core State Standards suggest that by eighth grade, students should be able to sketch graphs from functions that have been described verbally.

This chapter begins with an introduction to the rectangular coordinate system, also called the Cartesian coordinate system (named for the ancient mathematician-philosopher Descartes,) or more simply called the xy-plane. It then explores certain aspects of the plane and finishes by graphing the linear equations explored in this chapter.

WHY? Objectives

Using the activities in this chapter, pre-algebra students:

- Consider and briefly express what is the most unclear concepts from a lesson
- Visualize and comprehend the significant parts of an algebraic graph: points, ordered pairs, intercepts, slope, and so forth

- Fill in a K-W-L chart that asks readers what they already know, what they want to know, and what they learned regarding a lesson or mathematical concept
- Complete a semantic feature analysis showing different ways of expressing graphing features and terms
- Complete an anticipation guide to explore and compare their and the text's knowledge of linear equations and graphs

Mini-Lesson 7.1   The xy-Plane and Lines

CCSS Standard 8.EE: Equations and Expressions

Understand the connections between proportional relationships, lines, and linear equations.

Before students begin creating graphs, they need to learn a few new algebraic concepts. First, consider a linear equation in two variables; for example, $y = x + 2$. The single-variable equations that we studied earlier had one variable and usually one solution; these new equations will have many solutions. These solutions take the form of ordered pairs: generally (x,y) or specifically, for example, $(2,4)$. Each linear equation in two variables has an infinite set of ordered pairs or solutions. All of the ordered pairs, which indicate points on a graph, lie on a straight line. Here are a few ordered pairs that are solutions to the example: $y = x + 2$ are $(0,2)$, $(1,3)$, and $(-2, 0)$.

We'll start with the *linear equation*: a linear equation in two variables $(x$ and $y)$ can be written in the form $AX + BY = C$ where A, B, and C are real numbers. But A and B cannot both equal 0.

Students will learn more about different forms of linear equations in future algebra courses. For now, we'll stick to the basics.

The next concept is the plane that will contain the graphs. Notice that the figure has four quadrants, I to IV, and that they are numbered in a counterclockwise order. The vertical bold line is the y-axis, and the horizontal bold line is the x-axis. The x-axis meets the y-axis at one point $(0,0)$ called the origin.

Ordered pairs are points where the horizontal $(y = k)$ and vertical $(x = m)$ grid lines intersect. The left value of the point (x,y) represents the x coordinate and the right value the y coordinate. For example, to plot the point $(-3, 2)$, move 3 units from the origin along the x-axis to the negative, and from there move 2 units up to the positive.

The following shows the graph of a line with corresponding equation $y - x = 2$:

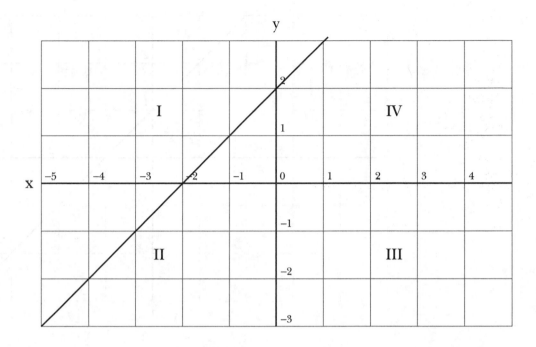

We know from geometry that it takes only two points and a straight edge or ruler to determine a line. The point $(-2, 0)$ sits on the x-axis and is called an *x-intercept*. The point $(0,2)$ sits on the y-axis and is called an *intercept*. $(-2, 0)$ and $(0,2)$ are solutions to the linear equation $y - x = 2$. Once we found these two points, we took a ruler and joined or sketched the line between the two intercepts and beyond them. Hence, we created the graph for the linear equation $y = x + 2$. Every point along this line is an ordered pair solution to the equation $y - x = 2$.

☀ Teaching Tip

Because it takes only two points to determine a line, students only need to find the x and y intercepts and join the two points to graph any linear equation. However, $y = x$ is the identity equation, and its x and y intercepts are the same point $(0,0)$. In this case, any other point on the line $y = x$ will do for the second point, such as $(2,2)$. Remember that it takes two points to make a line!

The linear equation represented by this line is y = 1 − x, with two intercepts: (0,1) and (1,0).

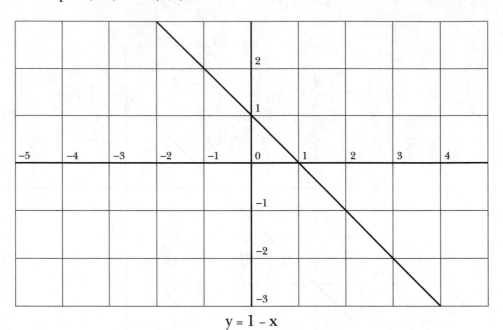

y = 1 - x

The following table lists several of the points on this line. It should be clear that the table would go on forever if we were to attempt to list all points on this line.

x	y
0	1
1	0
2	−1
−1	2
−2	3
$\frac{1}{2}$	$\frac{1}{2}$
3	−2

Activity 7.1 Muddiest Point

$2x - 5x + 6x = 3x$ $A(B + C) = AB + AC$ $4 \times 5 = 5 \times 4$ $2(3 + 5)^2 + (-1)^2$ $y = mx + b$

WHAT? Description

The muddiest point (Angelo & Cross, 1993) activity allows teachers to assess student comprehension of the content addressed in a classroom discussion or lesson. Students are given an index card or worksheet 7.1 at the end of the day's lesson and asked to jot down the topic they found most confusing. Also have them write out the topic they found easiest or simplest to grasp. Students hand in their cards as they leave the classroom. Often the cards will reveal one or two topics that several students found unclear and also where they understood the content. This point or points of confusion may be addressed in the next lesson or, if time permits, a review of these topics may become the next lesson.

WHY? Objectives

During this activity, pre-algebra students:

- Choose and write out the most unclear topic for them from the day's lesson
- Identify parts of the lesson they understood

HOW? Examples

Here is an example of a student's response to the muddiest and clearest parts of a lesson on linear equations in two variables and their graphs:

For me the muddiest topics in this unit are:

- x and y intercepts
- slopes
- constructing lines
- slope intercept form

For me the easiest topics in this unit are:

- plotting points
- parallel and perpendicular lines
- writing equations in slope intercept form

Worksheet 7.1 Muddiest Point

NAME _____   DATE _____

$$2x - 5x + 6x = 3x \quad A(B + C) = AB + AC \quad 4 \times 5 = 5 \times 4 \quad 2(3 + 5)^2 + (-1)^2 \quad y = mx + b$$

The muddiest point presented in class today is:

_____

_____

_____

_____

_____

The easiest thing presented in class today was:

_____

_____

_____

_____

_____

_____

Pre-Algebra Out Loud

Activity 7.2 Reading and Understanding Graphs

$2x - 5x + 6x = 3x \quad A(B + C) = AB + AC \quad 4 \times 5 = 5 \times 4 \quad 2(3 + 5)^2 + (-1)^2 \quad y = mx + b$

WHAT? Description

The National Council of Teachers of Mathematics (2010) holds that it is vital for students to be able to interpret as well as create graphical representations of mathematical relations. Today computers and graphing calculators allow students to visualize and manipulate graphs of quantitative relationships. The latest technological tools include interactive graphs with sliders and other gauges that allow users to change variable values, which in turn change the graph. These tools allow students to see how the changes in the independent variable affect the dependent variable and the shape of the graph.

The prerequisites for interpreting graphs include understanding the basics of graphing and two-variable equations. Students who are introduced to graphing early seem to grasp better the notion of function. Notice how your students seem to like and often use the vertical line test to tell if a graph represents a function. Every time a student says, "It passes the vertical line test," offer the opportunity to reinforce what that statement means (each x has exactly one y).

Once students have an understanding of variables, ordered pairs, intercepts, and axes, they are ready to examine and interpret graphical models. To interpret a graph, students should first read any headings or captions around the graph. Then they should refer to the graphical model and ask and answer as many of the following questions that are applicable to this particular graph. Using complete sentences will help students to clarify and complete their thoughts:

- What does the independent variable (x) represent in real-world terms?
- What does the dependent variable (y) represent?
- What does it mean when the y value = 0?
- What does it mean when the x value = 0?
- If x = [pick a value], what is y? What does this point represent?
- If the graph is linear, what does the slope of the line represent?

During this activity, pre-algebra students:

- Learn about the xy-plane and graphs
- Write about the graphic model and what are its attributes
- Explore higher-level graphs

HOW? Example

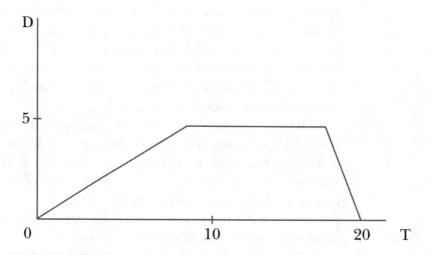

This graph represents the distance D (the number of blocks) that Brandylee walks from her home and back. The T-axis represents the time in minutes that passes as she walks.

If the highest point of the graph is D = 5, then it takes 10 minutes for Brandylee to walk 5 blocks from home. Her speed is D ÷ T = 5 ÷ 10 = 1 ÷ 2, which means she walked at a rate of 1 block per 2 minutes or 1.5 blocks per minute.

From 10 to 20 minutes, she does not walk, so she must have rested for 10 minutes. Then it looks as if she jogged home quickly, taking about 2 minutes. She ran the 5 blocks home in 2 minutes, so her speed was 2.5 blocks per minute.

The entire journey from home and back happened in 22 minutes.

Worksheet 7.2 Reading and Understanding Graphs

NAME _____   DATE _____

$2x - 5x + 6x = 3x$ $A(B + C) = AB + AC$ $4 \times 5 = 5 \times 4$ $2(3 + 5)^2 + (-1)^2$ $y = mx + b$

Directions: Consider the following graph of Gabriel walking in his neighborhood. Let D = distance in blocks from home and T represent the time in minutes.

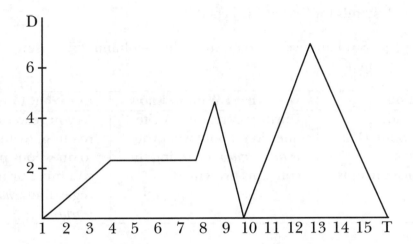

On another sheet of paper, answer the following questions using clear, complete sentences:

- In your own words, write out what the D variable represents.
- In your own words, write out what the T variable represents.
- When T = 0, what does D equal? Write out what this means in terms of time and distance.
- When T = 4 minutes, how far is Gabriel from home?
- What are the basic shapes of the graph?
- Is distance a function of time in this graph?
- The graph changes at what points? How do these points represent Gabriel's walk?
- What is Gabriel doing at T = 4 through T = 7 seconds?
- There are three points where D = 0. What does each point represent in terms of Gabriel's distance from home and time passed during his walk?
- Can you determine the speed of Gabriel's walk at T = 2, T = 5, T = 8, and T = 10 in blocks per minute?

In a paragraph describe Gabriel's walk as depicted by this graph. Feel free to be creative and embellish the story if you wish.

Activity 7.3 K-W-L

WHAT? Description

K-W-L (Ogle, 1986) is a reading strategy that uses note taking prior to, during, and after reading:

K stands for "What I **K**now"
W stands for "What I **W**ant to Know"
L stands for "What I **L**earned"

Students write notes in a three-column grid using the following format:

K—What I Know	W—What I Want to Know	L—What I Learned
During prereading, write notes about what you *already know* regarding the concepts presented.	During prereading, write questions about what you *want to know* regarding the concepts presented.	As you read or after reading, write answers to questions posed in column 2 or notes regarding *what you have learned.*

WHY? Objectives

During this activity, pre-algebra students:

- Reflect on prior and new knowledge
- Merge prior knowledge with new knowledge
- Summarize prior and new knowledge
- Authentically assess [self-assess] their own learning process

HOW? Example

The concept is graphing a line. A student might fill in the table as shown below:

K—What I Know	W—What I Want to Know	L—What I Learned
A graph of a line has many points on it.	Where do you get the points from?	The points are ordered pairs like (x,y) that make the equation work!

Worksheet 7.3 K-W-L

NAME _____   DATE _____

Directions: The K-W-L reading strategy follows this format:

K—What I Know	W—What I Want to Know	L—What I Learned
During prereading, write notes about what you *already know* regarding the concepts presented.	During prereading, write questions about what you *want to know* regarding the concepts presented.	As you read or after reading, write answers to questions posed in column 2 or notes regarding *what you have learned.*

Use the reading titled _____

on page _____ to complete this table:

K—What I Know	W—What I Want to Know	L—What I Learned

Worksheet 7.4 K-W-L for the Slope of a Line

NAME _____   DATE _____

$2x - 5x + 6x = 3x$ $A(B + C) = AB + AC$ $4 \times 5 = 5 \times 4$ $2(3 + 5)^2 + (-1)^2$ $y = mx + b$

Directions: The K-W-L reading strategy follows this format:

K—What I Know	W—What I Want to Know	L—What I Learned
During prereading, write notes about what you *already know* regarding the concepts presented.	During prereading, write questions about what you *want to know* regarding the concepts presented.	As you read or after reading, write answers to questions posed in column 2 or notes regarding *what you have learned.*

Use the reading titled _____
on page _____ to complete this table:

K—What I Know	W—What I Want to Know	L—What I Learned

Pre-Algebra Out Loud

CCSS Standard 8.EE: Expressions and Equations

Understand the connections between proportional relationships, lines, and linear equations.

Every linear equation with two variables has a slope, that is, the measure of the slant or steepness of the line. By convention, the variable m usually is used to refer to the slope, a numerical measure of the slant of a line. If a graph descends from left to right, like the one below, it will have a negative slope. Graphs that descend from left to right will have a positive slope. The slope is also the comparison of the difference in Y's to the difference in X's.

Slope Formulas

$$m = \frac{rise}{run} = \frac{\Delta y}{\Delta x} = \frac{y_2 - y_1}{x_2 - x_2}$$

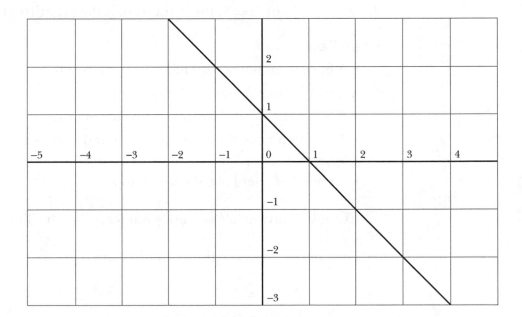

☀ Teaching Tip

Lines that descend from left to right have negative slopes, and ones that ascend from left to right have positive slopes.

The x intercept of the line in the preceding graph is the point (1,0). The y intercept is the point (0,1). The slope of the line can be found using the slope formula and is −1.

$$M = \Delta x - \Delta y = 0 - 1 - 1 - 0 = -1$$

 ## Teaching Tip

Refrain from using the expression "no slope." Some texts consider a line with no slope to be a horizontal line. Other texts use the phrase to mean the slope does not exist, as in the case of any vertical line. To avoid confusion, tell your students not to use it at all.

Consider another form of the linear equation, the slope intercept form. The slope intercept form of a linear equation is y = mx + b, where m is the slope and b is the y intercept. When these ideas are put together, the equation for the line in the preceding graph is y = −x + 1. Since the slope m = −1 and b = 1, the y intercept is the point (0,1).

Slope Facts

- A horizontal line always has a slope of m = 0.
- A vertical line has an undefined slope.
- A steep line has a slope much greater than 1.
- A line that goes through the origin and bisects the xy plane has a slope of 1.
- All parallel lines have the same slope.

Example: Find the slope and y intercept for the line with equation 2x − y = 6.

First, rewrite the equation into slope intercept form:

$$-2x - y = 6$$
$$2x - y + 2x = 6 + 2x$$
$$-y = 6 + 2x$$

Dividing both sides by −1 gives

$$y = -2x - 6$$

The equation is now in slope intercept form. It can easily be seen that the slope is −2 and the y intercept b = −6.

Activity 7.4 Semantic Feature Analysis

$$2x - 5x + 6x = 3x \quad A(B + C) = AB + AC \quad 4 \times 5 = 5 \times 4 \quad 2(3 + 5)^2 + (-1)^2 \quad y = mx + b$$

WHAT? Description

Semantic feature analysis (Baldwin, Ford, & Readance, 1981) is a reading strategy that asks students to complete a matrix showing how various terms and concepts are alike or different. The matrix itself consists of several columns. The first lists the terms, and the other columns contain headings spelling out features that the terms or concepts might have in common.

WHY? Objectives

During this activity, pre-algebra students:

- Explore features of certain mathematical concepts
- Compare and contrast features of related mathematical concepts
- Summarize this information
- Refer back to the completed matrix when reviewing for exams

HOW? Example

In this table on semantic feature analysis for slope, students were asked to fill in the table by writing yes or no to the questions along the top of the table for the types of slope given in column 1. Then for column 6, they sketched the line and its correct slant. The "yes" answers are given.

	Line Ascends?	Line Descends?	Horizontal Line?	Vertical Line?	Sketch Line with Slope
Positive slope	yes				
Negative slope		yes			
Zero slope			yes		
Undefined slope				yes	

Worksheet 7.5 Semantic Feature Analysis: Linear Equations

NAME _____ DATE _____

$2x - 5x + 6x = 3x$ $A(B + C) = AB + AC$ $4 \times 5 = 5 \times 4$ $2(3 + 5)^2 + (-1)^2$ $y = mx + b$

Directions: Beginning with each equation in the first column, answer each question across the top. If no solution exists, write "DNE" (for "does not exist").

Linear Equation	Give the slope	Give the y intercept in (0, y) form	Does the line ascend or descend from left to right?	Give the x intercept in (0, x) form
$y = 2x - 6$				
$2x - 4y = 8$				
$x + y = 9$				
$y = 4x$				

Worksheet 7.6 Semantic Feature Analysis: Slope

NAME _____ DATE _____

2x − 5x + 6x = 3x   A(B + C) = AB + AC   4 × 5 = 5 × 4   2(3 + 5)² + (−1)²   y = mx + b

Directions: Beginning with each equation in the first column, answer each question across the top. If no solution exists, write "DNE" (for "does not exist").

Equation	Write in slope intercept form $y = mx$	Give the slope	Give the y intercept	Write in standard form: $ax + by = c$
Contains (2,5) and (−1, 0)				
Horizontal line through the point (0,3)				
Vertical line through the point (3,0)				
Identity equation				
Passes through (0,2) and (−3, 0)				

Activity 7.5 Anticipation Guide

$2x - 5x + 6x = 3x \quad A(B + C) = AB + AC \quad 4 \times 5 = 5 \times 4 \quad 2(3 + 5)^2 + (-1)^2 \quad y = mx + b$

WHAT? Description

Anticipation guides (Herber, 1978) are lists of statements that challenge students to explore their knowledge of concepts prior to reading the text.

A mathematical anticipation guide usually contains four to five statements, each with two parts. First, students are asked to agree or disagree with each statement. Then they are asked to read the text and determine whether the text or author agrees with each statement.

WHY? Objectives

During this activity, pre-algebra students:

- Complete anticipation charts
- Explore their opinions and prior knowledge of mathematical concepts
- Read closely to find evidence to support their claims or discover the text's view
- Uncover and identify any misconceptions regarding these concepts

HOW? Example

This example is an anticipation guide for a lesson on slope. Students were directed to put a check mark in the Me column next to any statement with which they agreed and a check mark next to any statement with which the text agreed:

Me	Text	
√		1. A slope is the measure of the slant or tilt of a line.
		2. A horizontal line has an undefined slope.
√	√	3. If a line falls from left to right, it will have a negative slope.
		4. Perpendicular lines never touch or cross each other.
√	√	5. The slope-intercept form for linear equations is $y = mx + b$.

Worksheet 7.7 Anticipation Guide: Planes, Lines, and Point

NAME _____   DATE _____

$$2x - 5x + 6x = 3x \quad A(B + C) = AB + AC \quad 4 \times 5 = 5 \times 4 \quad 2(3 + 5)^2 + (-1)^2 \quad y = mx + b$$

Directions: Consider the lesson on linear equations and slope Then in the column labeled Me, place a check next to any statement with which you agree. After reading the section, consider the column labeled Text, and place a check next to any statement with which the text agrees.

Me	Text	
		A plane is a flat surface that goes on and on forever in all directions.
		Any line that goes through the point (0,0) will have a slope of 0.
		x intercepts are of the form (k,0) where k is any real number. _____
		y intercepts are also of the form (k,0) where n is a real number.
		All linear equations can be written in the form $Ax + By = C$ where A, B, and C are real numbers, not all 0.

Worksheet 7.8 Anticipation Guide: Linear Equations

NAME _____   DATE _____

$$2x - 5x + 6x = 3x \quad A(B + C) = AB + AC \quad 4 \times 5 = 5 \times 4 \quad 2(3 + 5)^2 + (-1)^2 \quad y = mx + b$$

Directions: Consider the lesson on linear equations and slope. Then in the column labeled Me, place a check next to any statement with which you agree. After reading the section, consider the column labeled Text, and place a check next to any statement with which the text agrees.

Me	Text	
		Another name for the xy-plane is the rectangular coordinate plane.
		Any line that goes through the point (0,0) will be the identity equation $y = x$.
		The equation $y = -2x + 6$ has a slope of -2 and y intercept $(0,6)$.
		The lines $y = 2x - 1$ and $y = \frac{1}{2} - x + 5$ are perpendicular to each other.
		The slope is the difference in x's divided by the difference in y's.

8

$$2x - 5x + 6x = 3x \quad y = mx + b$$

Geometry

WHAT? Introduction

The first number systems were developed by the Egyptians and Babylonians some four thousand years ago. Around 400 to 300 B.C., the ancient Greeks became the masters of mathematics, believing that the only way to prove a rule to be true was to use a straightedge (ruler without number marks) and a compass (which was often a piece of rope wrapped around a twig or a stone). For this reason, we think of the Greeks as the discoverers of geometry.

In this chapter, we first explore plane figures: rectangles, circles, triangles, and other two-dimensional figures. According to the Common Core State Standards, fifth-grade students are expected to be able to classify these figures into categories based on their basic properties. The second mini-lesson introduces two of the three-dimensional solids: pyramids and prisms.

WHY? Objectives

Using the activities in this chapter, pre-algebra students:

- Understand and explain various significant features of plane figures
- Complete a semantic feature analysis chart showing and comparing the different features of plane figures

- Write out a method of operation for solving geometry problems
- Create a math story using geometric terms from a lesson
- Learn to paraphrase math content
- Research and write biographies of famous geometers

Mini-Lesson 8.1   Plane Figures

CCSS Standard 7.6: Geometry

Draw, construct, and describe geometrical figures and describe the relationships between them.

In geometry, two-dimensional figures are called *plane figures* because they are sketched on a flat area. Plane figures have the following properties:

- They are closed sketches made of line segments with sides or curves with no gaps. The following square and circle are plane figures:

- Plane figures are also convex: any line segment drawn inside the plane figure will not go outside and back in. The first figure is convex, and the second one is not. Because the line segment is not completely contained in the second figure, the second figure is not convex; rather, it is concave.

Pre-Algebra Out Loud

• Polygons are closed, convex figures with line segments for sides. Generally these figures are called n-gons, where "n" is a prefix for the number of sides: five sides for a pentagon, six to a hexagon, seven for a heptagon, and so on. However, a 3-gon is called a triangle, and a 4-gon is a quadrilateral.

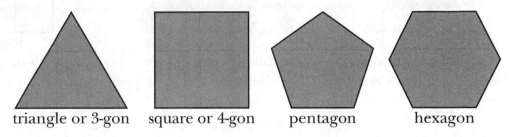

triangle or 3-gon   square or 4-gon   pentagon   hexagon

• Quadrilaterals (4-gons) are a special class of polygons. Each has its own set of special properties. (See the semantic feature analysis activity in this chapter.)

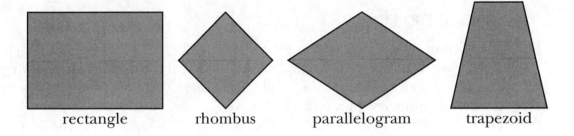

rectangle   rhombus   parallelogram   trapezoid

• Circular plane figures are all related to the circle and have curves in place of line segments.

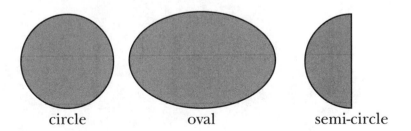

circle   oval   semi-circle

• Triangles (3-gons) have several variations. Three are shown below.

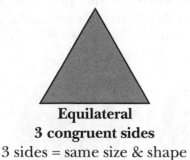 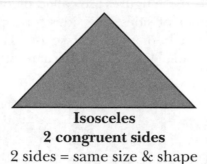 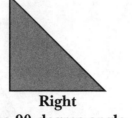

Equilateral	**Isosceles**	**Right**
3 congruent sides	**2 congruent sides**	**one 90-degree angle**
3 sides = same size & shape	2 sides = same size & shape	acute (all other angles < 90°)

• An equilateral triangle is called a regular triangle. Any n-gon with all congruent sides is said to be regular.

Students who understand these basic shapes will find learning higher-level geometry much simpler.

 Teaching Tip

Regular polygons have a lot of symmetry. Have students cut an isosceles, equilateral, and several other triangles out of paper or card stock. If a line can be found where the triangle folds exactly on top of itself, you have found a line of symmetry. Try finding all the lines of symmetry for a regular hexagon.

Activity 8.1 Geometric Figure Description

WHAT? Description

This activity encourages students to reflect on and choose appropriate terms to describe the specific features of a geometric figure, increasing their geometric vocabulary in the process. First, sketch two different geometric figures and make copies for each student. Divide students into two groups of equal size. Each student in each group is given a copy of one of the figures to observe and write a description of on a separate sheet of paper. They then trade their descriptions with the members of the opposite group. Each student attempts to sketch the figure based on the written description he or she receives. The original version of the geometric figure is then viewed and students are encouraged to discuss their descriptions and sketches in pairs.

WHY? Objectives

During this activity, pre-algebra students:

- Sketch the described figure when given written descriptions of a geometric figure
- Discuss their misunderstandings or how they understood with their partners after completing the activity

HOW? Examples

The following example shows a plane figure and three descriptions of the figure. These are the directions:

Write out a description of the given figure in at least two complete sentences. Use language that your peers will understand and from which they will be able to sketch the figure. Then you and your partner trade descriptions of your figure and try to sketch the figure using the description.

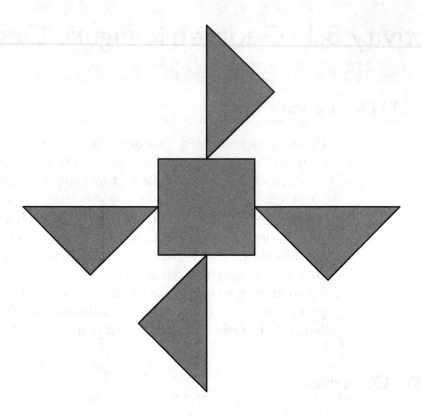

These are three students' descriptions and the teacher's rating for each:

Student 1's description: This is a two-dimensional figure. It has a square in the middle of the figure and 4 triangles of equal size and shape coming out of each side. Each triangle meets the side of the square at one vertex.

Teaching's rating: GOOD. This description works because it uses the correct geometric forms and refers to place and size of all shapes. However, the 4 triangles could be explained further. They are right triangles.

Student 2's description: There is a large square in the center of the drawing. Around the square are right triangles that are about one-half of the size of the center square. The triangles are attached to the middle of the sides of the square and each seems to be rotated about 90 degrees compared to the prior one.

Teacher's rating: VERY GOOD. This description is excellent, as it refers to all of the figures accurately and goes into great detail about the position of the triangles.

Student 3's description: This is a picture of a propeller with 4 blades around a square. Each blade meets each side of the square at a corner. The blades are smaller than the square.

Teacher's rating: POOR. This description is vague and nearly impossible to use to accurately sketch the figure.

Worksheet 8.1 Geometric Figure Description Activity

NAME _____   DATE _____

Directions: Consider the three-dimensional figure here. On a separate sheet of paper, write out a description of the figure. Choose your vocabulary carefully so that another student can use your written description to sketch the image. When you are finished, trade your description with another student.

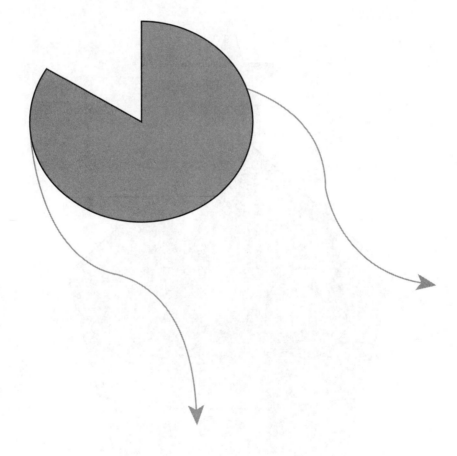

Geometry   **163**

Worksheet 8.2 Geometric Figure Description Activity

NAME _____ DATE _____

Directions: Consider the three-dimensional figure below. On a separate sheet of paper, write out a description of the figure. Choose your vocabulary carefully so that another student can use your written description to sketch the image. When you are finished, trade your description with another student.

Pre-Algebra Out Loud

Activity 8.2 Semantic Feature Analysis

WHAT? Description

Semantic feature analysis (Baldwin, Ford, & Readance, 1981) is a reading strategy that asks students to complete a matrix showing how various terms and concepts are alike or different. The terms or concepts are related or fall under a particular category. The matrix itself consists of several columns. The first column contains a listing of the terms. The remaining columns contain headings spelling out features that the terms or concepts might have in common.

This activity lends itself nicely to geometric figures because they have many easily understood features or parts. Usually the list of figures is in the first column of the matrix. Across the top, different yet related features can be placed in the first row of cells.

WHY? Objectives

During this activity, pre-algebra students:

- Compare and contrast features of related mathematical concepts
- Summarize this information
- Refer back to the completed matrix when reviewing for exams

HOW? Example

The table shows an example of a completed semantic feature analysis:

	Number of Sides	Number of 90-Degree Angles?	Number of Acute (Less Than 90 Degrees) Angles?	Number of Obtuse (Greater Than 90 Degrees) Angles?
Regular triangle	3	0	3	0
Regular quadrilateral	4	4	0	0
Regular pentagon	5	0	0	5

Worksheet 8.3 Semantic Feature Analysis

NAME _____   DATE _____

$$2x - 5x + 6x = 3x \quad A(B + C) = AB + AC \quad 4 \times 5 = 5 \times 4 \quad 2(3 + 5)^2 + (-1)^2 \quad y = mx + b$$

Directions: Answer yes or no to each question for each of the different figures regarding the sides of each 4-gon given in the first column. The first column has been completed for you.

Quadrilateral	All Sides Congruent?	Opposite Sides Congruent?	Opposite Sides Parallel?	Exactly One Pair of Parallel Sides?
Square	*yes*			
Rectangle	*no*			
Parallelogram	*no*			
Rhombus	*yes*			
Trapezoid	*no*			

Worksheet 8.4 Semantic Feature Analysis

NAME _____   DATE _____

Regular n-gons are polygons with n number of sides where all angles and sides of each n-gon are congruent. Remember that "congruent" means the figures are the same size and same shape.

Directions: Using the triangle in the first row as a model, fill in each cell following the directions in the column headings. When you get to the last regular n-gon, your last cell should be a formula that will give the measure of the vertex angles for each regular polygon.

Regular n-gons	Sketch	Number of interior triangles	Sum of all angles' degrees	Subtract 360 degrees	Divide by number of interior angles	Measure of interior angle
3-gon triangle		3	$3(180) = 540$	$540 - 360 = 180$	$\dfrac{180}{3}.$	60 degrees
4-gon square						
5-gon pentagon						
6-gon hexagon						
8-gon octagon						
n-gon						

CCSS Standard 7.G: Geometry

Draw, construct, and describe geometrical figures and express the relationships between them.

Many of the solids used in our everyday lives are in the shapes of pyramids and prisms. Both pyramids and prisms are polyhedra (the plural for *polyhedron*), meaning all their faces are polygons. In this lesson, we compare and contrast the two primary groups of solids: prisms and pyramids.

A *pyramid* has a polygonal base and triangular sides that form a vertex. A right pyramid has a base that is a polygon and determines the name of the pyramid. A square right pyramid has a square base. For example, the Great Pyramid in Egypt is a supersized-square pyramid.

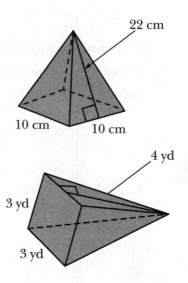

The world is full of three-dimensional objects; in fact, nearly all things are three-dimensional objects. In terms of polyhedra, pyramids and prisms in particular, we pack mail, toys, storage items, and gifts in boxes, or rectangular prisms. We can find rocks and plants that are roughly pyramid shaped. And buildings, artwork, and decorations often are either pyramids or prisms. As your students study more geometry, they will find many other three-dimensional figures.

A *prism* has two parallel and congruent polygonal faces. Its lateral (side) faces are rectangles. If the prism is a right prism, each rectangular side meets the polygonal face (also called *base*) at right angles. The number of sides of the polygonal faces give the name of the prism. For example, a square, or "right" prism, has two square faces and four rectangular sides. A hexagonal right prism has two hexagonal faces and six rectangular sides.

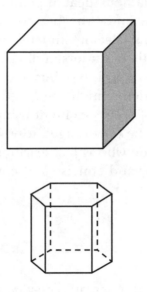

☀ Teaching Tip

Ask your students to break up into small groups and discuss what they think symmetry in a three-dimensional shape would look like.

Activity 8.3 Writing a Method of Operation

$2x - 5x + 6x = 3x$ $A(B + C) = AB + AC$ $4 \times 5 = 5 \times 4$ $2(3 + 5)^2 + (-1)^2$ $y = mx + b$

WHAT? Description

Most mathematical or geometric content consists of processes. Students need to know the how-tos, or methods, for arriving at or simplifying solutions. Having students write out methods of operation (MO) reinforces their understanding of how to solve problems and helps them consider the fine points of exceptions to the rule.

Students might be asked to write out the MO for finding the midpoint of a line segment using only a straightedge and a compass. They should be encouraged to write out the MO as if they were talking to a classmate who is just learning this process. This motivates the writer to be clear and concise and consider the geometric vocabulary he or she should know.

WHY? Objectives

During this activity, pre-algebra students:
- Complete a method of operation for a geometric process
- Use a completed MO to conduct a geometric process
- Share their MOs with their peers (optional)

HOW? Example

For this activity, you could ask students to do the following:
- Write out the MO for finding the area of any triangle.
- Write out the MO for finding all lines of reflection symmetry of a regular octagon.
- Research and find the method President Garfield invented in 1876 for proving the Pythagorean theorem. Then write out the MO for this proof in your own words.

Example of a Student MO

MO for finding the circumference of a circle with radius of 4 inches. The formula for the circumference is $C = 2\pi r$.

1. Decide on the accuracy you require for π, such as let $\pi = 3.14$.
2. Apply the formula: multiply $2 \times (3.14) \times 4 = 50.24$.
3. Consider the correct label or unit of measurement: in^2.
4. Give the complete solution, $C = 50.24\ in^2$.

Worksheet 8.5 offers a method of operations of a Pythagorean theorem proof.

 Teaching Tip

The Pythagorean formula is $a^2 + b^2 = c^2$, where a, b, and c, respectively, are the two legs and hypotenuse of a right triangle. The Pythagorean formula is one of the most significant and most proven formulas since the era of Greek mathematics, around 500 to 200 B.C. In his twentieth-century book, *The Pythagorean Proposition*, E. S. Loomis (1968) gives 370 proofs for the Pythagorean theorem.

Worksheet 8.5 Dissection Proof of the Pythagorean Formula

NAME _____   DATE _____

A proof is another type of method of operations. It gives the steps for the process you are demonstrating and adds the reasons that each step is accurate.

   Directions: Follow the directions (the MO for the proof of the Pythagorean formula) to show a unique proof. Use another sheet of paper for your proof.

1. Sketch an acute right triangle, labeling a and b as the length of the legs and c as the length of the hypotenuse.

2. Sketch a square off your triangle's hypotenuse where one side of the square is the hypotenuse of your triangle. Label all lengths of all sides c.

3. Sketch three more right triangles congruent to the original triangle, placing each with c as a side of the square. Again, label all sides. You should end up with a square with sides of length a + b. You may have to rearrange the four triangles to get them in the correct places. Remember that you need to end up with a large square with each side of the square having a length of a + b.

4. Set up an algebraic equation with the left side being $(a + b)^2 = $ _____. You will need to fill in the blank. *Hint:* You will need to use the formula for area of a triangle for part of this equation. Solve and see if you end up with $a^2 + b^2 = c^2$. If you do, you have successfully proven the Pythagorean theorem. Congratulations!!

   Find another geometric proof for the Pythagorean theorem. Write out the proof in your own words, using sketches when you need to. Remember that there are at least 370 of these proofs.

Worksheet 8.6 Methods of Operation for Constructions

NAME _____ DATE _____

$$2x - 5x + 6x = 3x \quad A(B + C) = AB + AC \quad 4 \times 5 = 5 \times 4 \quad 2(3 + 5)^2 + (-1)^2 \quad y = mx + b$$

Directions: Consider a line segment, AB:

A●————————————————————————————————————●B

    Write out the steps for finding the perpendicular bisector of AB using a compass and a straightedge. Use sketches to support your steps. Explain each step as you would to another student who missed this lesson. Two steps are given to get you started.

1. Place the point of the compass on the left end point of the line segment AB and open the compass to the length of AB. Draw an arc.
2. Write out the steps for constructing an equilateral triangle. Use sketches to support your steps.

A●————————————————————————————————————●B

Worksheet 8.7 Method of Operation for Finding Sum of Degrees of a Triangle

NAME _____   DATE _____

Directions: You will need a sheet of paper, scissors, and a ruler for this activity.

1. The sum of the measure of all three angles in any triangle is 180 degrees. Therefore, think of other geometric concepts that have that same measure. Some of these might be a straight angle, half the measure of the sum of all central angles of a circle, or the measure of the central angles off the diameter of a circle.

2. How might you use sketches to construct the congruence of these examples and the three angles of a triangle?

3. Consider placing the three angles next to each other to see if they form a straight angle.

4. Sketch several different-sized triangles with different angle measures, such as 30, 60, and 90 degrees or 45, 45, and 90 degrees.

5. Cut each corner of the triangle, with each cut-out showing the angle and its measure.

6. Place each of the cut-out angles next to each other. Do they form a straight angle of 180 degrees?

7. Will this work for all triangles? Write what you think here:

   _____

   _____

   _____

8. Explain why you think it will work all the time.

   _____

   _____

   _____

9. Have you proven this above? Why or why not?

   _____

   _____

   _____

10. What is the sum of all four angles of any quadrilaterals? Can you use the work above to explain why this is true?

   _____

   _____

   _____

Activity 8.4 Math Story

WHAT? Description

For this activity, give students a list of terms or concepts specific to geometry, and ask them to use all of the terms correctly to write a short story. This activity may be used during or after the lesson containing the specified terms. Asking students to use this language requires that they learn the meaning of these terms.

Students are encouraged to be creative, but also to pay close attention to the meanings of the geometrical terms. Their stories may be fiction or nonfiction; they may be witty, silly, sad, or dramatic. Be sure to give them some guidelines to follow when writing their stories. Being explicit about what constitutes an A paper is equally important to the student writer and the teacher reader-grader.

WHY? Objectives

During this activity, pre-algebra students:

- Write a short story using the geometric terms on the worksheet
- Follow all directions and use a dictionary or text to find definitions that you need
- Consider what each geometric term means.

HOW? Example

Example assignment: Write a brief math story using the following terms correctly: *pyramid, prism, edge, vertex, volume,* and *surface area.*

Jasmine and Jeff are very competitive and have decided to build two treehouses. Jasmine thinks a square prism would be the best shape for her house, but Jeff thinks a square pyramid would be better.

Both decided to draw a sketch to scale of their treehouse first. As they worked, they decided that the square base of each house would be a square 4 feet by 4 feet, which is 16 square feet. So each edge of the base would be 4 feet, and each angle at the 4 vertices of the base would be 90 degrees.

Geometry   **175**

Before they started building, they decided to compare the surface area of each house so they could find out whose house needed more paint. Without actually computing the surface area of each, Jasmine pointed out that since her treehouse had six squares that were 4 by 4 feet and Jeff's had only one square and four triangles meeting at a vertex top, it would take much more paint for the prism. Then they realized they must compute the volume of each because that would show how much living space each house would contain.

They found that the volume of the square prism, a cube, was 4 cubed, or 64 cubic feet. Jeff knew that to find the volume of his pyramid, he only had to find $\frac{1}{3}$ of the cube, which was $\frac{64}{3}$ cubic feet!

After all of this hard work, they decided maybe they should put their two solids together to form a square pyramid atop a cube!

They also decided to take a rest before they started building their treehouse.

Worksheet 8.8 Write Your Own Math Story

NAME _____ DATE _____

$2x - 5x + 6x = 3x$ $A(B + C) = AB + AC$ $4 \times 5 = 5 \times 4$ $2(3 + 5)^2 + (-1)^2$ $y = mx + b$

Directions: Use the following guidelines when you write your short story.

1. Be sure your story contains all the listed terms (see the box below).

2. Use each term correctly. Use the text or dictionary to check on definitions and correct usage of terms. You may be creative with each term, but in at least one place use the term correctly or in a manner that clearly demonstrates what the term means.

3. Your story may be fiction or nonfiction.

4. Your story should contain an introduction, conclusion, and follow a logical story line.

5. Your story should be between one and two pages in length.

6. Be creative, and choose a theme that has relevance to you.

Terms

Circle	Radius
Pi	Diameter
Chord	Tangent
Secant	Circumference
Area	Central angle
Inscribed angle	

Worksheet 8.9 Write Your Own Math Story

NAME _____ DATE _____

$$2x - 5x + 6x = 3x \quad A(B + C) = AB + AC \quad 4 \times 5 = 5 \times 4 \quad 2(3 + 5)^2 + (-1)^2 \quad y = mx + b$$

Directions: Use the following guidelines when you write your short story.

1. Be sure your story contains all the listed terms (see the box below).

2. Use each term correctly. Use the text or dictionary to check on definitions and correct usage of terms. You may be creative with each term, but in at least one place use the term correctly or in a manner that clearly demonstrates what the term means.

3. Your story may be fiction or nonfiction.

4. Your story should contain an introduction and conclusion, and follow a logical story line.

5. Your story should be between one and two pages in length.

6. Be creative, and choose a theme that has relevance to you.

Geometric Terms

Line	Point
Angle	Plane
Parallel	Perpendicular
Bisect	Midpoint
Median	Line segment
Right angle	Straight angle

Activity 8.5 In Your Own Words: A Paraphrasing Activity

$2x - 5x + 6x = 3x \quad A(B + C) = AB + AC \quad 4 \times 5 = 5 \times 4 \quad 2(3 + 5)^2 + (-1)^2 \quad y = mx + b$

WHAT? Description

One of the most common excuses that students give for not reading material in their textbook is that they do not understand the language. This activity helps students target and interpret key concepts. By rewriting mathematical passages, students demystify and make personal meaning of mathematical content.

Assign students small portions of the pre-algebra text to read and rewrite in their own words. This activity works equally well with concept definitions, theorems, and examples. Having students read their own versions to each other allows student writers to consider different interpretations and pinpoint misconceptions. If writing is handed in, you can assess your students' understanding of the material.

To extend the activity, allow students to use sketches of geometric shapes as a part of the paraphrasing exercise.

WHY? Objectives

During this activity, pre-algebra students:

• Paraphrase the content of assigned portions of the text
• Share their completed paraphrase handouts with their classmates

HOW? Example

Example assignment: Read the following paragraph about regular polyhedra and paraphrase (write in your own words) what it says:

Regular polyhedra are three-dimensional solids that have convex polygonal faces "Regular" means that all faces are the same size and shape. There are only five regular polyhedra, and they are called the "Platonic solids." Individually, they are a cube, tetrahedron, duodecahedron, and icosohedron. Plato, who lived around 300 B.C., knew that these were the only regular polyhedral and used mind-pictures to prove this to himself.

This is one student's curious paraphrase:

Some solids are easy to imagine, like the cube. Plato used his imagination to see that these 5 are the only solids that had all the same size and shape faces. A six-sided dice is a cube, and a calendar can be placed on a duodecahedron because it has 12 pentagonal faces and can sit upright on any face.

Worksheet 8.10 In Your Own Words: A Paraphrasing Activity

NAME _____ DATE _____

Directions: Read the passage below. Then write out your definition of an equilateral triangle. Be clear and use at least two complete sentences. Be prepared to share your definition with your peers. You may use other sources to help develop your definition.

An equilateral triangle is a triangle with three sides of equal length or three congruent (same size and same shape) sides. By using the following theorem, we can show that all equilateral triangles are equiangular.

Theorem: The two base angles of an isosceles triangle with the congruent sides meeting at the apex (top vertex) of the triangle are congruent.

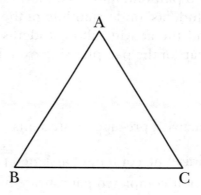

Your definition of an equilateral triangle:

_____

_____

_____

For extra credit, use another sheet of paper to write out your interpretation of the theorem, using A, B, and C for the angles and AB, AC, and BC for the sides. Then write out or show that an equilateral triangle is also equiangular. You may include sketches and words.

Pre-Algebra Out Loud

Activity 8.6 Biographies of Geometers

WHAT? Description

In 350 B.C. Euclid wrote the Elements, which details his axiomatic geometry based on the undefined terms *points*, *lines*, and *planes*, five postulates (assumptions), and more than 200 theorems. Each of the theorems is based on the undefined terms, postulates, and the theorems that came before the theorem in question. A theorem is a mathematical statement that can be proved to be true.

Researching a geometer's life and geometric contributions helps students understand the background and the step-by-step development of the various geometries and geometric processes. Several of the mathematicians and their contributions to the field of geometry are listed below. Students may be assigned a particular geometer or choose one of their liking. Also, having students peer-teach about their geometer is an excellent way to disseminate this knowledge to your class.

Geometers	Contributions
Pythagoras	Geometric proofs
Euclid	Euclidean geometry
Erastosthenes	Good approximation of the circumference of the Earth at the equator
Archimedes	Considered greatest mathematical genius of antiquity; volume of the sphere; physics
René Descartes	Cartesian coordinate system
Nicolai Lobachevsky	Non-Euclidean geometry (hyperbolic geometry)
Carl Frederick Gauss	Hyperbolic geometry
John Bolyai	Hyperbolic geometry
Berheim Riemann	Non-Euclidean geometry (spherical or elliptical geometry)
Jacob Steiner	Projective geometry
Hermann Minkowski	Taxicab metric

The research, writing, and sharing of a biography of a mathematician who contributed to the development of geometry helps students consider how and why the field of geometry came about. The development of geometry, like any other field of mathematics, is a step-by-step process of discovery and invention.

The assignment of a biography of a mathematician should include the format for the write-up. For example, each biography might consist of the following parts:

- Early life
- Education and career
- Family or social life
- Mathematical contributions
- Later life

WHY? Objectives

During this activity, pre-algebra students:

- Research a mathematician of their choosing and take notes
- Prepare a write-up of a mathematician's life story

HOW? Example

Grading

Content score = 1   2   3   4   5
   ◦ Contains all required parts?
   ◦ Contains accurate information?

Mechanics score = 1   2   3   4   5
   ◦ Grammar, spelling, clarity, transitions, introduction, conclusion?
   ◦ Follows guidelines?

Resources score = 1   2   3   4   5
   ◦ Format? Number of sources? Library source?

Final grade = 1   2   3   4   5

Worksheet 8.11 Math Biographies

$$2x - 5x + 6x = 3x \quad A(B + C) = AB + AC \quad 4 \times 5 = 5 \times 4 \quad 2(3 + 5)^2 + (-1)^2 \quad y = mx + b$$

Directions: Write a four- or five-page biography of one of the following mathematicians:

Geometers	Contributions
Pythagoras	Geometric proofs
Euclid	Euclidean geometry
Erastosthenes	Good approximation of the circumference of the Earth at the equator
Archimedes	Considered greatest mathematical genius of antiquity; volume of the sphere; physics
René Descartes	Cartesian coordinate system
Lobachevsky	Non-Euclidean geometry (hyperbolic geometry)
Gauss	Hyperbolic geometry
Bolyai	Hyperbolic geometry
Riemann	Non-Euclidean geometry (spherical or elliptical geometry)
Jacob Steiner	Projective geometry
Hermann Minkowski	Taxicab metric

Guidelines

1. The biography must contain the following parts of your mathematician's life:
   - Early life
   - Education and career
   - Family or social life
   - Geometric contributions
   - Later life
   - Resources
2. Use at least three different sources, one of them from the school's library.
3. Word-process the biography.
4. It should be a minimum of 4 pages and maximum of 6 pages in length.
5. The last page should be a bibliography of your sources in a consistent format.
6. End with your mathematician's influence on the field of geometry.

$$2x - 5x + 6x = 3x \quad A(B + C) = AB + AC \quad 4 \times 5 = 5 \times 4 \quad 2(3 + 5)^2$$

References

Angelo, T. A., & Cross, P. K. (1993). *Classroom assessment techniques: A handbook for college teachers* (2nd ed.). San Francisco: Jossey-Bass.

Baldwin, R. S., Ford, J. C., & Readance, J. E. (1981). Teaching word connotations: An alternative strategy. *Reading World, 21,* 103–108.

Barron, R. F. (1969). The use of vocabulary as advance organizer. In H. L. Herber & P. L. Sanders (Eds.), *Research in reading in the content areas: Third year report.* Syracuse, NY: Syracuse University, Reading and Language Arts Center.

Blachowicz, C. (1986). Making connections: Alternatives to the vocabulary notebook. *Journal of Reading, 29,* 643–649.

Common Core State Standards Initiative. (2011). *About the standards.* http://www.core standards.org/about-the-standards

Frayer, D. A., Frederick, W. C., & Klausmeier, H. J. (1969). *A schema for testing the level of concept mastery* (Tech. Rep. No. 16). Madison: University of Wisconsin, Research and Development Center for Cognitive Learning.

Herber, H. (1978). *Teaching reading in content areas* (2nd ed.). Upper Saddle River, NJ: Prentice Hall.

National Council of Teachers of Mathematics. (2010). *Principles and standards for school mathematics.* Reston, VA: National Council of Teachers of Mathematics.

Ogle, D. M. (1986). The Know, Want to Know learning strategy. In K. D. Muth (Ed.), *Children's comprehension of text* (pp. 205–223). Newark, DE: International Reading Association.

Vacca, R. T., & Vacca, J. L. (1999). *Content area reading* (6th ed.). Reading, MA: Addison-Wesley.